Ravindranath Tagore

GITANJALI

Ravindranath Tagore

GITANJALI

[Edited with Introduction, Author's Information, Complete Text, Summary and Analysis and Study Questions]

Misha Kandhari
M.A., M. Phil. English,
Delhi University

ANMOL PUBLICATIONS PVT. LTD.
NEW DELHI - 110 002 (INDIA)

ANMOL PUBLICATIONS PVT. LTD.

H.O.: 4374/4B, Ansari Road, Darya Ganj,
New Delhi-110 002 (India)
Ph.: 23278000, 23261597

B.O.: No. 1015, Ist Main Road, BSK IIIrd Stage
IIIrd Phase, IIIrd Block
Bangalore - 560 085 (India)
Visit us at: www.anmolpublications.com

Gitanjali

First Published, 2009

PRINTED IN INDIA

Printed at Balaji Offset Press, Delhi.

Contents

Preface

Bengali Indian writer. He translated into English his own verse *Gitanjali/Song Offerings* (1912) and his verse play *Chitra* (1896). He was awarded the Nobel Prize for Literature in 1913.

Born in Calcutta, into a wealthy family, he began to write poetry as a child; his first book appeared when he was only 17 years old. After studying law in England, he returned to India, where he was probably the most important and popular author of the colonial era, writing poetry, short stories, novels, and plays. An ardent nationalist and advocate of social reform, he resigned his knighthood as a gesture of protest against British repression in India

Chapter 1

Introduction

Rabindranath Tagore (1861-1941) was the youngest son of Debendranath Tagore, a leader of the Brahmo Samaj, which was a new religious sect in nineteenth-century Bengal and which attempted a revival of the ultimate monistic basis of Hinduism as laid down in the *Upanishads*. He was educated at home; and although at seventeen he was sent to England for formal schooling, he did not finish his studies there. In his mature years, in addition to his many-sided literary activities, he managed the family estates, a project which brought him into close touch with common humanity and increased his interest in social reforms. He also started an experimental school at Shantiniketan where he tried his Upanishadic ideals of education. From time to time he participated in the Indian nationalist movement, though in his own non-sentimental and visionary way; and Gandhi, the political father of modern India, was his devoted friend. Tagore was knighted by the ruling British Government in 1915, but within a few years he resigned the honour as a protest against British policies in India.

Tagore had early success as a writer in his native Bengal. With his translations of some of his poems he became rapidly known in the West. In fact his fame attained a luminous height, taking him across continents on lecture tours and tours of friendship. For the world he became the voice of India's spiritual heritage; and for India, especially for Bengal, he became a great living institution.

Although Tagore wrote successfully in all literary genres, he was first of all a poet. Among his fifty and odd volumes of poetry are *Manasi* (1890) [The Ideal One], *Sonar Tari* (1894) [The Golden Boat], *Gitanjali* (1910) [Song Offerings], *Gitimalya* (1914) [Wreath of Songs], and *Balaka* (1916) [The Flight of Cranes]. The English renderings of his poetry, which include *The Gardener* (1913), *Fruit-Gathering* (1916), and *The Fugitive* (1921), do not generally correspond to particular volumes in the original Bengali; and in spite of its title, *Gitanjali: Song Offerings* (1912), the most acclaimed of them, contains poems from other works besides its namesake. Tagore's major plays are *Raja* (1910) [*The King of the Dark Chamber*], *Dakghar* (1912) [*The Post Office*], *Achalayatan* (1912) [The Immovable], *Muktadhara* (1922) [The Waterfall], and *Raktakaravi* (1926) [*Red Oleanders*]. He is the author of several volumes of short stories and a number of novels, among them *Gora* (1910), *Ghare-Baire* (1916) [*The Home and the World*], and *Yogayog* (1929) [Crosscurrents]. Besides these, he wrote musical dramas, dance dramas, essays of all types, travel diaries, and two autobiographies, one in his middle years and the other shortly before his death in 1941. Tagore also left numerous drawings and paintings, and songs for which he wrote the music himself. Rabindranath Tagore was born in Calcutta, India into a wealthy Brahmin family. After a brief stay in England (1878) to attempt to study law, he returned to India, and instead pursued a career as a writer, playwright, songwriter, poet, philosopher and educator. During the first 51 years of his life he achieved some success in the Calcutta area of India where he was born and raised with his many stories, songs and plays. His short stories were published monthly in a friend's magazine and he even played the lead role in a few of the public performances of his plays. Otherwise, he was little known outside of the Calcutta area, and not known at all outside of India.

This all suddenly changed in 1912. He then returned to England for the first time since his failed attempt at law school as a teenager. Now a man of 51, his was accompanied by his son. On the way over to England he began translating, for the first time, his latest selections of poems, Gitanjali, into English. Almost all of his work prior to that time had been written in his native tongue of Bengali. He decided to do this just to have something to do, with no expectation at all that his first time translation efforts would be any good. He made the handwritten translations in a little notebook he carried around with him and worked on during the long sea voyage from India. Upon arrival, his son left his father's brief case with this notebook in the London subway. Fortunately, an honest person turned in the briefcase and it was recovered the next day. Tagore's one friend in England, a famous artist he had met in India, Rothenstein, learned of the translation, and asked to see it. Reluctantly, with much persuasion, Tagore let him have the notebook. The painter could not believe his eyes. The poems were incredible. He called his friend, W.B. Yeats, and finally talked Yeats into looking at the hand scrawled notebook.

The rest, as they say, is history. Yeats was enthralled. He later wrote the introduction to Gitanjali when it was published in September 1912 in a limited edition by the India Society in London. Thereafter, both the poetry and the man were an instant sensation, first in London literary circles, and soon thereafter in the entire world. His spiritual presence was awesome. His words evoked great beauty. Nobody had ever read anything like it. A glimpse of the mysticism and sentimental beauty of Indian culture were revealed to the West for the first time. Less than a year later, in 1913, Rabindranath received the Nobel Prize for literature. He was the first non-westerner to be so honored. Overnight he was famous and began world lecture tours promoting inter-cultural harmony and understanding. In 1915 he was knighted by the British King George V. When not traveling he remained at his family home outside of Calcutta, where he remained very active as a literary, spiritual and social-political force.

In 1919, following the Amritsar massacre of 400 Indian demonstrators by British troops, Sir Tagore renounced his Knighthood. Although a good friend of Mohandas Karamchand Gandhi, most of the time Tagore stayed out of politics. He was opposed to nationalism and miltiarism as a matter of principle, and instead promoted spiritual values and the creation of a new world culture founded in multi-culturalism, diversity and tolerance. He served as a spiritual and creative beacon to his countrymen, and indeed, the whole world. He used the funds from his writing and lecturing to expand upon the school he had founded in 1901 now known as Visva Bharati. The alternative to the poor system of education imposed by the British, combined the best of traditional Hindu education with Western ideals. Tagore's multi-cultural educational efforts were an inspiration to many, including his friend, Count Hermann Keyserling of Estonia. Count Keyserling founded his own school in 1920 patterned upon Tagore's school, and the ancient universities which existed in Northern India under Buddhist rule over 2,000 years ago under the name School of Wisdom. Rabindranath Tagore led the opening programme of the School of Wisdom in 1920, and participated in several of its programs thereafter.

Rabindranath Tagore's creative output tells you a lot about this renaissance man. The variety, quality and quantity are unbelievable. As a writer, Tagore primarily worked in Bengali, but after his success with Gitanjali, he translated many of his other works into English. He wrote over one thousand poems; eight volumes of short stories; almost two dozen plays and play-lets; eight novels; and many books and essays on philosophy, religion, education and social topics. Aside from words and drama, his other great love was music, Bengali style. He composed more than two thousand songs, both the music and lyrics. Two of them became the national anthems of India and Bangladesh. In 1929 he even began painting. Many of his paintings can be found in museums today, especially in India, where he is considered the greatest literary figure of India of all times.

Tagore was not only a creative genius, he was a great man and friend to many. For instance, he was also a good friend from childhood to the great Indian Physicist, Bose. He was educated and quite knowledgeable of Western culture, especially Western poetry and Science. This made him a remarkable person, one of the first of our planet to combine East and West, and ancient and modern knowledge. Tagore had a good grasp of modern - post-Newtonian - physics, and was well able to hold his own in a debate with Einstein in 1930 on the newly emerging principles of quantum mechanics and chaos. His meetings and tape recorded conversations with his contemporaries such Albert Einstein and H.G. Wells, stand as cultural landmarks, and show the brilliance of this great man. Although Tagore is a superb representative of his country - India - the man who wrote its national anthem - his life and works go far beyond his country. He is truly a man of the whole Earth, a product of the best of both traditional Indian, and modern Western cultures. The School of Wisdom is proud to have him as part of its heritage. He exemplifies the ideals important to us of Goodness, Meaningful Work, and World Culture.

Travels

Tagore (centre, at right) visits Chinese academics at Tsinghua University in 1924.

Owing to his notable wanderlust, between 1878 and 1932, Tagore visited more than thirty countries on five continents;many of these trips were crucial in familiarising non-Indian audiences to his works and spreading his political ideas. In 1912, he took a sheaf of his translated works to England, where they impressed missionary and Gandhi protégé Charles F. Andrews, Anglo-Irish poet William Butler Yeats, Ezra Pound, Robert Bridges, Ernest Rhys, Thomas Sturge Moore, and others.Indeed, Yeats wrote the preface to the English translation of Gitanjali, while Andrews joined Tagore at Santiniketan. On 10 November 1912, Tagore toured the United States and the United Kingdom, staying in Butterton, Staffordshire with Andrews' clergymen friends. From 3 May 1916 until April 1917, Tagore went on lecturing circuits in Japan and the United States, during which he denounced nationalism—particularly that of the Japanese and Americans. He also wrote the essay "Nationalism in India", attracting both derision and praise (the latter from pacifists, including Romain Rolland). Shortly after returning to India, the 63-year-old Tagore visited Peru at the invitation of the Peruvian government, and took the opportunity to visit Mexico as well. Both governments pledged donations of

$100,000 to the school at Shantiniketan (Visva-Bharati) in commemoration of his visits. A week after his November 6, 1924 arrival in Buenos Aires, Argentina, an ill Tagore moved into the Villa Miralrío at the behest of Victoria Ocampo. He left for India in January 1925. On 30 May 1926, Tagore reached Naples, Italy; he met fascist dictator Benito Mussolini in Rome the next day. Their initially warm rapport lasted until Tagore spoke out against Mussolini on 20 July 1926.

Tagore (first row, third figure from right) meets members of the Iranian Majlis (Tehran, April-May 1932). Tagore visited Shiraz in the same year,.

On 14 July 1927, Tagore and two companions began a four-month tour of Southeast Asia, visiting Bali, Java, Kuala Lumpur, Malacca, Penang, Siam, and Singapore. Tagore's travelogues from the tour were collected into the work "Jatri".In early 1930 he left Bengal for a nearly year-long tour of Europe and the United States. Once he returned to the UK, while his paintings were being exhibited in Paris and London, he stayed at a Friends settlement in Birmingham. There, he wrote his Hibbert Lectures for the University of Oxford (which dealt with the "idea of the humanity of our God, or the divinity of Man the Eternal") and spoke at London's annual Quaker gathering. There (addressing relations between the British and Indians, a topic he would grapple with over the next two years), Tagore spoke of a "dark chasm of aloofness". He later visited Aga Khan III, stayed at Dartington Hall, then toured Denmark, Switzerland, and Germany from June to mid-September 1930, then the Soviet Union. Lastly, in April 1932, Tagore—who was acquainted with the legends and works of the Persian mystic Hafez—was invited as a personal guest of Shah Reza Shah Pahlavi of Iran. Such extensive travels allowed Tagore to interact with many notable contemporaries, including Henri Bergson, Albert Einstein, Robert Frost, Thomas Mann, George Bernard Shaw, H.G. Wells and Romain Rolland Tagore's last travels abroad, including visits to Persia and Iraq (in 1932) and Ceylon in 1933, only sharpened his opinions regarding human divisions and nationalism.

Chapter 2

Tagore and His India

Voice of Bengal

Rabindranath Tagore, who died in 1941 at the age of eighty, is a towering figure in the millennium-old literature of Bengal. Anyone who becomes familiar with this large and flourishing tradition will be impressed by the power of Tagore's presence in Bangladesh and in India. His poetry as well as his novels, short stories, and essays are very widely read, and the songs he composed reverberate around the eastern part of India and throughout Bangladesh.

In contrast, in the rest of the world, especially in Europe and America, the excitement that Tagore's writings created in the early years of the twentieth century has largely vanished. The enthusiasm with which his work was once greeted was quite remarkable. *Gitanjali,* a selection of his poetry for which he was awarded the Nobel Prize in Literature in 1913, was published in English translation in London in March of that year, and had been reprinted ten times by November, when the award was announced. But he is not much read now in the West, and already by 1937, Graham Greene was able to say: "As for Rabindranath Tagore, I cannot believe that anyone but Mr. Yeats can still take his poems very seriously."

The Mystic

The contrast between Tagore's commanding presence in Bengali literature and culture, and his near-total eclipse in the rest of the world, is perhaps less interesting than the distinction between the view of Tagore as a deeply relevant and many-sided contemporary thinker in Bangladesh and India, and his image in the West as a repetitive and remote spiritualist. Graham Greene had, in fact, gone on to explain that he associated Tagore "with what Chesterton calls 'the bright pebbly eyes' of the Theosophists."Certainly, an air of mysticism played some part in the "selling" of Rabindranath Tagore to the West by Yeats, Ezra Pound, and his other early champions. Even Anna Akhmatova, one of Tagore's few later admirers (who translated his poems into Russian in the mid-1960s), talks of "that mighty flow of poetry which takes its strength from Hinduism as from the Ganges, and is called Rabindranath Tagore."

Confluence of Cultures

Rabindranath did come from a Hindu family—one of the landed gentry who owned estates mostly in what is now Bangladesh. But whatever wisdom there might be in Akhmatova's invoking of Hinduism and the Ganges, it did not prevent the largely Muslim citizens of Bangladesh from having a deep sense of identity with Tagore and his ideas. Nor did it stop the newly independent Bangladesh from choosing one of Tagore's songs—the "Amar Sonar Bangla" which means "my golden Bengal"—as its national anthem.

This must be very confusing to those who see the contemporary world as a "clash of civilizations"—with "the Muslim civilization," "the Hindu civilization," and "the Western civilization," each forcefully confronting the others. They would also be confused by Rabindranath Tagore's own description of his Bengali family as the product of "a confluence of three cultures:

Hindu, Mohammedan, and British". Rabindranath's grandfather, Dwarkanath, was well known for his command of Arabic and Persian, and Rabindranath grew up in a family atmosphere in which a deep knowledge of Sanskrit and ancient Hindu texts was combined with an understanding of Islamic traditions as well as Persian literature. It is not so much that Rabindranath tried to produce—or had an interest in producing—a "synthesis" of the different religions (as the great

Moghul emperor Akbar tried hard to achieve) as that his outlook was persistently non-sectarian, and his writings—some two hundred books—show the influence of different parts of the Indian cultural background as well as of the rest of the world.

Abode of Peace

Most of his work was written at Santiniketan (Abode of Peace), the small town that grew around the school he founded in Bengal in 1901, and he not only conceived there an imaginative and innovative system of education, but through his writings and his influence on students and teachers, he was able to use the school as a base from which he could take a major part in India's social, political, and cultural movements.

The profoundly original writer, whose elegant prose and magical poetry Bengali readers know well, is not the sermonizing spiritual guru admired—and then rejected—in London. Tagore was not only an immensely versatile poet; he was also a great short story writer, novelist, playwright, essayist, and composer of songs, as well as a talented painter whose pictures, with their mixture of representation and abstraction, are only now beginning to receive the acclaim that they have long deserved. His essays, moreover, ranged over literature, politics, culture, social change, religious beliefs, philosophical analysis, international relations, and much else. The coincidence of the fiftieth anniversary of Indian independence with the publication of a selection of Tagore's letters by Cambridge University Press brought Tagore's ideas and reflections to the fore, which makes it important to examine what kind of leadership in thought and understanding he provided in the Indian subcontinent in the first half of this century.

Gandhi and Tagore

Since Rabindranath Tagore and Mohandas Gandhi were two leading Indian thinkers in the twentieth century, many commentators have tried to compare their ideas. On learning of Rabindranath's death, Jawaharlal Nehru, then incarcerated in a British jail in India, wrote in his prison diary for August 7, 1941: "Gandhi and Tagore. Two types entirely different from each other, and yet both of them typical of India, both in the long line of India's great men... It is not so much because of any single virtue but because of the *tout ensemble*, that I felt that among the world's great men today Gandhi and Tagore were supreme as human beings. What good fortune for me to have come into close contact with them."

Romain Rolland was fascinated by the contrast between them, and when he completed his book on Gandhi, he wrote to an Indian academic, in March 1923: "I have finished my *Gandhi*, in which I pay tribute to your two great river-like souls, overflowing with divine spirit, Tagore and Gandhi." The following month, he recorded in his diary an account of some of the differences between Gandhi and Tagore written by Reverend C.F. Andrews, the English clergyman and public activist who was a close friend of both men (and whose important role in Gandhi's life in South Africa as well as India is well portrayed in Richard Attenborough's film Gandhi [1982]). Andrews described to Rolland a discussion between Tagore and Gandhi, at which he was present, on subjects that divided them:

"The first subject of discussion was idols; Gandhi defended them, believing the masses incapable of raising themselves immediately to abstract ideas. Tagore cannot bear to see the people eternally treated as a child. Gandhi quoted the great things achieved in Europe by the flag as an idol; Tagore found it easy to object, but Gandhi held his ground, contrasting European flags bearing eagles, etc., with his own, on which he has put a spinning wheel. The second point of discussion was nationalism, which Gandhi defended. He said that one must go through nationalism to reach internationalism, in the same way that one must go through war to reach peace." Tagore greatly admired Gandhi but he had many disagreements with him on a variety of subjects, including nationalism, patriotism, the importance of cultural exchange, the role of rationality and of science, and the nature of economic and social development. These differences, I shall argue, have a clear and consistent pattern, with Tagore pressing for more room for reasoning, and for a less traditionalist view, a greater interest in the rest of the world, and more respect for science and for objectivity generally. Rabindranath knew that he could not have given India the political leadership that Gandhi provided, and he was never stingy in his praise for what Gandhi did for the nation (it was, in fact, Tagore who popularized the term "Mahatma"—great soul—as a description of Gandhi). And yet each remained deeply critical of many things that the other stood for.

That Mahatma Gandhi has received incomparably more attention outside India and also within much of India itself makes it important to understand "Tagore's side" of the Gandhi-Tagore debates. In his prison diary, Nehru wrote: "Perhaps it is as well that [Tagore] died now and did not see the many horrors that are likely to descend in increasing measure on the world and on India. He had seen enough and he was infinitely sad and unhappy." Toward the end of his life, Tagore was indeed becoming discouraged about the state of India, especially as its normal burden of problems, such as hunger and poverty, was being supplemented by politically organized incitement to "communal" violence between Hindus and Muslims.

This conflict would lead in 1947, six years after Tagore's death, to the widespread killing that took place during partition; but there was much gore already during his declining days. In December 1939, he wrote to his friend Leonard Elmhirst, the English philanthropist and social reformer who had worked closely with him on rural reconstruction in India (and who had gone on to found the Dartington Hall Trust in England and a progressive school at Dartington that explicitly invoked Rabindranath's educational ideals): "It does not need a defeatist to feel deeply anxious about the future of millions who, with all their innate culture and their peaceful traditions are being simultaneously subjected to hunger, disease, exploitations foreign and indigenous, and the seething discontents of communalism."

How would Tagore have viewed the India of today?

Would he see progress there, or wasted opportunity, perhaps even a betrayal of its promise and conviction? And, on a wider subject, how would he react to the spread of cultural separatism in the contemporary world?

East and West

Given the vast range of his creative achievements, perhaps the most astonishing aspect of the image of Tagore in the West is its narrowness; he is recurrently viewed as "the great mystic from the East," an image with a putative message for the West, which some would welcome, others dislike, and still others find deeply boring. To a great extent this Tagore was the West's own creation, part of its tradition of message-seeking from the East, particularly from India, which—as Hegel put it—had "existed for millennia in the imagination of the Europeans." Friedrich Schlegel, Schelling, Herder, and Schopenhauer were only a few of the thinkers who followed the same pattern. They theorized, at first, that India was the source of superior wisdom. Schopenhauer at one stage even argued that the New Testament "must somehow be of Indian origin: this is attested by its completely Indian ethics, which transforms morals into asceticism, its pessimism, and its avatar," in "the person of Christ." But then they rejected their own theories with great vehemence, sometimes blaming India for not living up to their unfounded expectations.

We can imagine that Rabindranath's physical appearance—handsome, bearded, dressed in non-Western clothes—may, to some extent, have encouraged his being seen as a carrier of exotic wisdom. Yasunari Kawabata, the first Japanese Nobel Laureate in Literature, treasured memories from his middle-school days of "this sage-like poet":

> His white hair flowed softly down both sides of his forehead; the tufts of hair under the temples also were long like two beards, and linking up with the hair on his cheeks, continued into his beard, so that he gave an impression, to the boy I was then, of some ancient Oriental wizard.

That appearance would have been well-suited to the selling of Tagore in the West as a quintessentially mystical poet, and it could have made it somewhat easier to pigeonhole him. Commenting on Rabindranath's appearance, Frances Cornford told William Rothenstein, "I can now imagine a powerful and gentle Christ, which I never could before." Beatrice Webb, who did not like Tagore and resented what she took to be his "quite obvious dislike of all that the Webbs stand for" (there is, in fact, little evidence that Tagore had given much thought to this subject), said that he was "beautiful to look at" and that "his speech has the perfect intonation and slow chant-like moderation of the dramatic saint." Ezra Pound and W. B. Yeats, among others, first led the chorus of adoration in the Western appreciation of Tagore, and then soon moved to neglect and even shrill criticism.

The contrast between Yeats's praise of his work in 1912 ("These lyrics...display in their thought a world I have dreamed of all my life long," "the work of a supreme culture") and his denunciation in 1935 ("Damn Tagore") arose partly from the inability of Tagore's many-sided writings to fit into the narrow box in which Yeats wanted to place—and keep—him. Certainly, Tagore did write a huge amount, and published ceaselessly, even in English (sometimes in indifferent English translation), but Yeats was also bothered, it is clear, by the difficulty of fitting Tagore's later writings into the image Yeats had presented to the West. Tagore, he had said, was the product of "a whole people, a whole civilization, immeasurably strange to us," and yet "we have met our own image,...or heard, perhaps for the first time in literature, our voice as in a dream."

Yeats did not totally reject his early admiration (as Ezra Pound and several others did), and he included some of Tagore's early poems in *The Oxford Book of Modern Verse,* which he edited in 1936. Yeats also had some favorable things to say about Tagore's prose writings. His censure of Tagore's later poems was reinforced by his dislike of Tagore's own English translations of his work ("Tagore does not know English, no Indian knows English," Yeats explained), unlike the English version of *Gitanjali* which Yeats had himself helped to prepare. Poetry is, of course, notoriously difficult to translate, and anyone who knows Tagore's poems in their original Bengali cannot feel satisfied with any of the translations (made with or without Yeats's help). Even the translations of his prose works suffer, to some extent, from distortion. E.M. Forster noted, in a review of a translation of one of Tagore's great Bengali novels, *The Home and the World*, in 1919: "The theme is so beautiful," but the charms have "vanished in translation," or perhaps "in an experiment that has not quite come off."

Tagore himself played a somewhat bemused part in the boom and bust of his English reputation. He accepted the extravagant praise with much surprise as well as pleasure, and then received denunciations with even greater surprise, and barely concealed pain. Tagore was sensitive to criticism, and was hurt by even the most far-fetched accusations, such as the charge that he was getting credit for the work of Yeats, who had "rewritten" Gitanjali. (This charge was made by a correspondent for The Times, Sir Valentine Chirol, whom E.M. Forster once described as "an old Anglo-Indian reactionary hack.") From time to time Tagore also protested the crudity of some of his overexcited advocates. He wrote to C.F. Andrews in 1920: "These people...are like drunkards who are afraid of their lucid intervals."

God and Others

Yeats was not wrong to see a large religious element in Tagore's writings. He certainly had interesting and arresting things to say about life and death. Susan Owen, the mother of Wilfred Owen, wrote to Rabindranath in 1920, describing her last conversations with her son before he left for the war which would take his life. Wilfred said goodbye with "those wonderful words of yours—beginning at 'When I go from hence, let this be my parting word.'" When Wilfred's pocket notebook was returned to his mother, she found "these words written in his dear writing—with your name beneath."

The idea of a direct, joyful, and totally fearless relationship with God can be found in many of Tagore's religious writings, including the poems of *Gitanjali*. From India's diverse religious traditions he drew many ideas, both from ancient texts and from popular poetry. But "the bright pebbly eyes of the Theosophists" do not stare out of his verses. Despite the archaic language of the original translation of *Gitanjali,* which did not, I believe, help to preserve the simplicity of the original, its elementary humanity comes through more clearly than any complex and intense spirituality:

Leave this chanting and singing and telling of beads! Whom dost thou worship in this lonely dark corner of a temple with doors all shut?

Open thine eyes and see thy God is not before thee!

He is there where the tiller is tilling the hard ground and where the pathmaker is breaking stones.

He is with them in sun and in shower, and his garment is covered with dust.

An ambiguity about religious experience is central to many of Tagore's devotional poems, and makes them appeal to readers irrespective of their beliefs; but excessively detailed interpretation can ruinously strip away that ambiguity. This applies particularly to his many poems which combine images of human love and those of pious devotion. Tagore writes:

I have no sleep to-night. Ever and again I open my door and look out on the darkness, my friend!

I can see nothing before me. I wonder where lies thy path!

By what dim shore of the ink-black river, by what far edge of the frowning forest, through what mazy depth of gloom, art thou threading thy course to come to see me, my friend?

I suppose it could be helpful to be told, as Yeats hastens to explain, that "the servant or the bride awaiting the master's home-coming in the empty house" is "among the images of the heart turning to God." But in Yeats's considerate attempt to make sure that the reader does not miss the "main point," something of the enigmatic beauty of the Bengali poem is lost - even what had survived the antiquated language of the English translation. Tagore certainly had strongly held religious beliefs (of an unusually nondenominational kind), but he was interested in a great many other things as well and had many different things to say about them.

Some of the ideas he tried to present were directly

political, and they figure rather prominently in his letters and lectures. He had practical, plainly expressed views about nationalism, war and peace, cross-cultural education, freedom of the mind, the importance of rational criticism, the need for openness, and so on. His admirers in the West, however, were tuned to the more otherworldly themes which had been emphasized by his first Western patrons. People came to his public lectures in Europe and America, expecting ruminations on grand, transcendental themes; when they heard instead his views on the way public leaders should behave, there was some resentment, particularly (as E.P. Thompson reports) when he delivered political criticism "at $700 a scold."

Reasoning in Freedom

For Tagore it was of the highest importance that people be able to live, and reason, in freedom. His attitudes toward politics and culture, nationalism and internationalism, tradition and modernity, can all be seen in the light of this belief. Nothing, perhaps, expresses his values as clearly as a poem in *Gitanjali:*

Where the mind is without fear
and the head is held high;
Where knowledge is free;
Where the world has not been
broken up into fragments
by narrow domestic walls;...
Where the clear stream of reason
has not lost its way into the
dreary desert sand of dead habit;...
Into that heaven of freedom,
my Father, let my country awake.

Rabindranath's qualified support for nationalist movements—and his opposition to the unfreedom of alien rule—came from this commitment. So did his reservations about patriotism, which, he argued, can limit both the freedom to engage ideas from outside "narrow domestic walls" and the freedom also to support the causes of people in other countries. Rabindranath's passion for freedom underlies his firm opposition to unreasoned traditionalism, which makes one a prisoner of the past (lost, as he put it, in "the dreary desert sand of dead habit").

Tagore illustrates the tyranny of the past in his amusing yet deeply serious parable "Kartar Bhoot" ("The Ghost of the Leader"). As the respected leader of an imaginary land is about to die, his panic-stricken followers request him to stay on after his death to instruct them on what to do. He consents. But his followers find their lives are full of rituals and constraints on everyday behavior and are not responsive to the world around them. Ultimately, they request the ghost of the leader to relieve them of his domination, when he informs them that he exists only in their minds.

Tagore's deep aversion to any commitment to the past that could not be modified by contemporary reason extended even to the alleged virtue of invariably keeping past promises. On one occasion when Mahatma Gandhi visited Tagore's school at Santiniketan, a young woman got him to sign her autograph book. Gandhi wrote: "Never make a promise in haste. Having once made it fulfill it at the cost of your life." When he saw this entry, Tagore became agitated. He wrote in the same book a short poem in Bengali to the effect that no one can be made "a prisoner forever with a chain of clay." He went on to conclude in English, possibly so that Gandhi could read it too, "Fling away your promise if it is found to be wrong."

Tagore had the greatest admiration for Mahatma Gandhi as a person and as a political leader, but he was also highly skeptical of Gandhi's form of nationalism and his conservative instincts regarding the country's past traditions. He never criticized Gandhi personally. In the 1938 essay, "Gandhi the Man," he wrote:

Great as he is as a politician, as an organizer, as a leader of men, as a moral reformer, he is greater than all these as a man, because none of these aspects and activities limits his humanity. They are rather inspired and sustained by it.

And yet there is a deep division between the two men. Tagore was explicit about his disagreement:

We who often glorify our tendency to ignore reason,

installing in its place blind faith, valuing it as spiritual, are ever paying for its cost with the obscuration of our mind and destiny. I blamed Mahatmaji for exploiting this irrational force of credulity in our people, which might have had a quick result [in creating] a superstructure, while sapping the foundation. Thus began my estimate of Mahatmaji, as the guide of our nation, and it is fortunate for me that it did not end there.

But while it "did not end there," that difference of vision was a powerful divider. Tagore, for example, remained unconvinced of the merit of Gandhi's forceful advocacy that everyone should spin at home with the "charka," the primitive spinning wheel. For Gandhi this practice was an important part of India's self-realization. "The spinning-wheel gradually became," as his biographer B.R. Nanda writes, "the centre of rural uplift in the Gandhian scheme of Indian economics." Tagore found the alleged economic rationale for this scheme quite unrealistic. As Romain Rolland noted, Rabindranath "never tires of criticizing the charka." In this economic judgment, Tagore was probably right. Except for the rather small specialized market for high-quality spun cloth, it is hard to make economic sense of hand-spinning, even with wheels less primitive than Gandhi's charka. Hand-spinning as a widespread activity can survive only with the help of heavy government subsidies. However, Gandhi's advocacy of the charka was not based only on economics. He wanted everyone to spin for "thirty minutes every day as a sacrifice," seeing this as a way for people who are better off to identify themselves with the less fortunate. He was impatient with Tagore's refusal to grasp this point:

The poet lives for the morrow, and would have us do likewise.... "Why should I, who have no need to work for food, spin?" may be the question asked. Because I am eating what does not belong to me. I am living on the spoliation of my countrymen. Trace the source of every coin that finds its way into your pocket, and you will realise the truth of what I write. Every one must spin. Let Tagore spin like the others. Let him burn his foreign clothes; that is the duty today. God will take care of the morrow.

If Tagore had missed something in Gandhi's argument, so did Gandhi miss the point of Tagore's main criticism. It was not only that the charka made little economic sense, but also, Tagore thought, that it was not the way to make people reflect on anything: "The charka does not require anyone to think; one simply turns the wheel of the antiquated invention endlessly, using the minimum of judgment and stamina."

Celibacy and Personal Life: Tagore and Gandhi's attitudes toward personal life were also quite different. Gandhi was keen on the virtues of celibacy, theorized about it, and, after some years of conjugal life, made a private commitment—publicly announced—to refrain from sleeping with his wife. Rabindranath's own attitude on this subject was very different, but he was gentle about their disagreements:

Gandhiji condemns sexual life as inconsistent with the moral progress of man, and has a horror of sex as great as that of the author of *The Kreutzer Sonata,* but, unlike Tolstoy, he betrays no abhorrence of the sex that tempts his kind. In fact, his tenderness for women is one of the noblest and most consistent traits of his character, and he counts among the women of his country some of his best and truest comrades in the great movement he is leading.

Tagore's personal life was, in many ways, an unhappy one. He married in 1883, lost his wife in 1902, and never remarried. He sought close companionship, which he did not always get (perhaps even during his married life—he wrote to his wife, Mrinalini: "If you and I could be comrades in all our work and in all our thoughts it would be splendid, but we cannot attain all that we desire"). He maintained a warm friendship with, and a strong Platonic attachment to, the literature-loving wife, Kadambari, of his elder brother, Jyotirindranath. He dedicated some poems to her before his marriage, and several books afterward, some after her death (she committed suicide, for reasons that are not fully understood, at the age of twenty-five, four months after Rabindranath's wedding).

Much later in life, during his tour of Argentina in 1924-1925, Rabindranath came to know the talented and beautiful

Victoria Ocampo, who later became the publisher of the literary magazine *Sur*. They became close friends, but it appears that Rabindranath deflected the possibility of a passionate relationship into a confined intellectual one. His friend Leonard Elmhirst, who accompanied Rabindranath on his Argentine tour, wrote:

Besides having a keen intellectual understanding of his books, she was in love with him—but instead of being content to build a friendship on the basis of intellect, she was in a hurry to establish that kind of proprietary right over him which he absolutely would not brook. Ocampo and Elmhirst, while remaining friendly, were both quite rude in what they wrote about each other. Ocampo's book on Tagore (of which a Bengali translation was made from the Spanish by the distinguished poet and critic Shankha Ghosh) is primarily concerned with Tagore's writings but also discusses the pleasures and difficulties of their relationship, giving quite a different account from Elmhirst's, and never suggesting any sort of proprietary intentions.

Victoria Ocampo, however, makes it clear that she very much wanted to get physically closer to Rabindranath: "Little by little he [Tagore] partially tamed the young animal, by turns wild and docile, who did not sleep, dog-like, on the floor outside his door, simply because it was not done." Rabindranath, too, was clearly very much attracted to her. He called her "Vijaya" (the Sanskrit equivalent of Victoria), dedicated a book of poems to her, Purabi—an "evening melody," and expressed great admiration for her mind ("like a star that was distant"). In a letter to her he wrote, as if to explain his own reticence:

When we were together, we mostly played with words and tried to laugh away our best opportunities to see each other clearly... Whenever there is the least sign of the nest becoming a jealous rival of the sky [,] my mind, like a migrant bird, tries to take... flight to a distant shore.

Five years later, during Tagore's European tour in 1930, he sent her a cable: "Will you not come and see me." She did. But their relationship did not seem to go much beyond conversation, and their somewhat ambiguous correspondence continued over the years. Written in 1940, a year before his death at eighty, one of the poems in Sesh Lekha ("Last Writings"), seems to be about her: "How I wish I could once again find my way to that foreign land where waits for me the message of love!/... Her language I knew not, but what her eyes said will forever remain eloquent in its anguish." However indecisive, or confused, or awkward Rabindranath may have been, he certainly did not share Mahatma Gandhi's censorious views of sex. In fact, when it came to social policy, he advocated contraception and family planning while Gandhi preferred abstinence.

Science and the People: Gandhi and Tagore severely clashed over their totally different attitudes toward science. In January 1934, Bihar was struck by a devastating earthquake, which killed thousands of people. Gandhi, who was then deeply involved in the fight against untouchability (the barbaric system inherited from India's divisive past, in which "lowly people" were kept at a physical distance), extracted a positive lesson from the tragic event. "A man like me," Gandhi argued, "cannot but believe this earthquake is a divine chastisement sent by God for our sins" in particular the sins of untouchability. "For me there is a vital connection between the Bihar calamity and the untouchability campaign."

Tagore, who equally abhorred untouchability and had joined Gandhi in the movements against it, protested against this interpretation of an event that had caused suffering and death to so many innocent people, including children and babies. He also hated the epistemology implicit in seeing an earthquake as caused by ethical failure. "It is," he wrote, "all the more unfortunate because this kind of unscientific view of [natural] phenomena is too readily accepted by a large section of our countrymen."

The two remained deeply divided over their attitudes toward science. However, while Tagore believed that modern science was essential to the understanding of physical phenomena, his views on epistemology were interestingly heterodox. He did not take the simple "realist" position often associated with modern science. The report of his conversation with Einstein, published in The New York Times in 1930, shows how insistent Tagore was on interpreting truth through observation and reflective concepts. To assert that something is true or untrue in the absence of anyone to observe or perceive its truth, or to form a conception of what it is, appeared to Tagore to be deeply questionable. When Einstein remarked, "If there were no human beings any more, the Apollo Belvedere no longer would be beautiful?" Tagore simply replied, "No." Going further—and into much more interesting territory—Einstein said, "I agree with regard to this conception of beauty, but not with regard to truth." Tagore's response was: "Why not? Truth is realized through men."

Tagore's epistemology, which he never pursued systematically, would seem to be searching for a line of reasoning that would later be elegantly developed by Hilary Putnam, who has argued: "Truth depends on conceptual schemes and it is nonetheless 'real truth.'" Tagore himself said little to explain his convictions, but it is important to take account of his heterodoxy, not only because his speculations were invariably interesting, but also because they illustrate how his support for any position, including his strong interest in science, was accompanied by critical scrutiny.

Nationalism and Colonialism: Tagore was predictably hostile to communal sectarianism (such as a Hindu orthodoxy that was antagonistic to Islamic, Christian, or Sikh perspectives). But even nationalism seemed to him to be suspect. Isaiah Berlin summarizes well Tagore's complex position on Indian nationalism: Tagore stood fast on the narrow causeway, and did not betray his vision of the difficult truth. He condemned romantic overattachment to the past, what he called the tying of India to the past "like a sacrificial goat tethered to a post," and he accused men who displayed it - they seemed to him reactionary - of not knowing what true political freedom was, pointing out that it is from English thinkers and English books that the very notion of political liberty was derived. But against cosmopolitanism he maintained that the English stood on their own feet, and so must Indians. In 1917 he once more denounced the danger of 'leaving everything to the unalterable will of the Master,' be he brahmin or Englishman. The duality Berlin points to is well reflected also in Tagore's attitude toward cultural diversity. He wanted Indians to learn what is going on elsewhere, how others lived, what they valued, and so on, while remaining interested and involved in their own culture and heritage. Indeed, in his educational writings the need for synthesis is strongly stressed. It can also be found in his advice to Indian students abroad. In 1907 he wrote to his son-in-law Nagendranath Gangulee, who had gone to America to study agriculture:

To get on familiar terms with the local people is a part of your education. To know only agriculture is not enough; you must know America too. Of course if, in the process of knowing America, one begins to lose one's identity and falls into the trap of becoming an Americanised person contemptuous of everything Indian, it is preferable to stay in a locked room.

Tagore was strongly involved in protest against the Raj on a number of occasions, most notably in the movement to resist the 1905 British proposal to split in two the province of Bengal, a plan that was eventually withdrawn following popular resistance. He was forthright in denouncing the brutality of British rule in India, never more so than after the Amritsar massacre of April 13, 1919, when 379 unarmed people at a peaceful meeting were gunned down by the army, and two thousand more were wounded. Between April 23 and 26, Rabindranath wrote five agitated letters to C.F. Andrews, who himself was extremely disturbed, especially after he was told by a British civil servant in India that thanks to this show of strength, the "moral prestige" of the Raj had "never been higher."

A month after the massacre, Tagore wrote to the Viceroy of India, asking to be relieved of the knighthood he had accepted four years earlier: The disproportionate severity of the punishments inflicted upon the unfortunate people and the methods of carrying them out, we are convinced, are without parallel in the history of civilized governments, barring some conspicuous exceptions, recent and remote. Considering that such treatment has been meted out to a population, disarmed and resourceless, by a power which has the most terribly efficient organisation for destruction of human lives, we must strongly assert that it can claim no political expediency, far less moral justification.... The universal agony of indignation roused in the hearts of our people has been ignored by our rulers - possibly congratulating themselves for imparting what they imagine as salutary lessons.... I for my part want to stand, shorn of all special distinctions, by the side of those of my countrymen who for their so-called insignificance are liable to suffer a degradation not fit for human beings.

Both Gandhi and Nehru expressed their appreciation of the important part Tagore took in the national struggle. It is fitting that after independence, India chose a song of Tagore ("Jana Gana Mana Adhinayaka," which can be roughly translated as "the leader of people's minds") as its national anthem. Since Bangladesh would later choose another song of Tagore ("Amar Sonar Bangla") as its national anthem, he may be the only one ever to have authored the national anthems of two different countries.

Tagore's criticism of the British administration of India was consistently strong and grew more intense over the years. This point is often missed, since he made a special effort to dissociate his criticism of the Raj from any denigration of British—or Western—people and culture. Mahatma Gandhi's well-known quip in reply to a question, asked in England, on what he thought of Western civilization ("It would be a good idea") could not have come from Tagore's lips. He would understand the provocations to which Gandhi was responding - involving cultural conceit as well as imperial tyranny. D.H. Lawrence supplied a fine example of the former: "I become more and more surprised to see how far higher, in reality, our European civilization stands than the East, Indian and Persian, ever dreamed of....

This fraud of looking up to them—this wretched worship-of-Tagore attitude is disgusting." But, unlike Gandhi, Tagore could not, even in jest, be dismissive of Western civilization. Even in his powerful indictment of British rule in India in 1941, in a lecture which he gave on his last birthday, and which was later published as a pamphlet under the title *Crisis in Civilization,* he strains hard to maintain the distinction between opposing Western imperialism and rejecting Western civilization. While he saw India as having been "smothered under the dead weight of British administration" (adding "another great and ancient civilization for whose recent tragic history the British cannot disclaim responsibility is China"), Tagore recalls what India has gained from "discussions centred upon Shakespeare's drama and Byron's poetry and above all...the large-hearted liberalism of nineteenth-century English politics." The tragedy, as Tagore saw it, came from the fact that what "was truly best in their own civilization, the upholding of dignity of human relationships, has no place in the British administration of this country." "If in its place they have established, baton in hand, a reign of 'law and order,' or in other words a policeman's rule, such a mockery of civilization can claim no respect from us."

Critique of Patriotism: Rabindranath rebelled against the strongly nationalist form that the independence movement often took, and this made him refrain from taking a particularly active part in contemporary politics. He wanted to assert India's right to be independent without denying the importance of what India could learn—freely and profitably—from abroad. He was afraid that a rejection of the West in favour of an indigenous Indian tradition was not only limiting in itself; it could easily turn into hostility to other influences from abroad, including Christianity, which came to parts of India by the fourth century; Judaism, which came through Jewish immigration shortly after the fall of Jerusalem, as did Zoroastrianism through Parsi immigration later on (mainly in the eighth century), and, of course—and most importantly—Islam, which has had a very strong presence in India since the tenth century.

Tagore's criticism of patriotism is a persistent theme in his writings. As early as 1908, he put his position succinctly in a letter replying to the criticism of Abala Bose, the wife of a great Indian scientist, Jagadish Chandra Bose: "Patriotism cannot be our final spiritual shelter; my refuge is humanity. I will not buy glass for the price of diamonds, and I will never allow patriotism to triumph over humanity as long as I live." His novel *Ghare Baire* (The Home and the World) has much to say about this theme. In the novel, Nikhil, who is keen on social reform, including women's liberation, but cool toward nationalism, gradually loses the esteem of his spirited wife, Bimala, because of his failure to be enthusiastic about anti-British agitations, which she sees as a lack of patriotic commitment. Bimala becomes fascinated with Nikhil's nationalist friend Sandip, who speaks brilliantly and acts with patriotic militancy, and she falls in love with him.

Nikhil refuses to change his views: "I am willing to serve my country; but my worship I reserve for Right which is far greater than my country. To worship my country as a god is to bring a curse upon it." As the story unfolds, Sandip becomes angry with some of his countrymen for their failure to join the struggle as readily as he thinks they should ("Some Mohamedan traders are still obdurate"). He arranges to deal with the recalcitrants by burning their meager trading stocks and physically attacking them. Bimala has to acknowledge the connection between Sandip's rousing nationalistic sentiments and his sectarian - and ultimately violent-actions. The dramatic events that follow (Nikhil attempts to help the victims, risking his life) include the end of Bimala's political romance.

This is a difficult subject, and Satyajit Ray's beautiful film of *The Home and the World* brilliantly brings out the novel's tensions, along with the human affections and disaffections of the story. Not surprisingly, the story has had many detractors, not just among dedicated nationalists in India. Georg Lukács found Tagore's novel to be "a petit bourgeois yarn of the shoddiest kind," "at the intellectual service of the British police," and "a contemptible caricature of Gandhi." It would, of course, be absurd to think of Sandip as Gandhi, but the novel gives a "strong and gentle" warning, as Bertolt Brecht noted in his diary, of the corruptibility of nationalism, since it is not even-handed. Hatred of one group can lead to hatred of others, no matter how far such feeling may be from the minds of large-hearted nationalist leaders like Mahatma Gandhi.

Admiration and Criticism of Japan: Tagore's reaction to nationalism in Japan is particularly telling. As in the case of India, he saw the need to build the self-confidence of a defeated and humiliated people, of people left behind by developments elsewhere, as was the case in Japan before its emergence during the nineteenth century. At the beginning of one of his lectures in Japan in 1916 ("Nationalism in Japan"), he observed that "the worst form of bondage is the bondage of dejection, which keeps men hopelessly chained in loss of faith in themselves." Tagore shared the admiration for Japan widespread in Asia for demonstrating the ability of an Asian nation to rival the West in industrial development and economic progress. He noted with great satisfaction that Japan had "in giant strides left centuries of inaction behind, overtaking the present time in its foremost achievement." For other nations outside the West, he said, Japan "has broken the spell under which we lay in torpor for ages, taking it to be the normal condition of certain races living in certain geographical limits."

But then Tagore went on to criticize the rise of a strong nationalism in Japan, and its emergence as an imperialist nation. Tagore's outspoken criticisms did not please Japanese audiences and, as E.P. Thompson wrote, "the welcome given to him on his first arrival soon cooled." Twenty-two years later, in 1937, during the Japanese war on China, Tagore received a letter from Rash Behari Bose, an anti-British Indian revolutionary then living in Japan, who sought Tagore's approval for his efforts there on behalf of Indian independence, in which he had the support of the Japanese government. Tagore replied:

Your cable has caused me many restless hours, for it hurts me very much to have to ignore your appeal. I wish you had asked for my cooperation in a cause against which my spirit did not protest. I know, in making this appeal, you counted on my great regard for the Japanese for I, along with the rest of Asia, did once admire and look up to Japan and did once fondly hope that in Japan Asia had at last discovered its challenge to the West, that Japan's new strength would be consecrated in safeguarding the culture of the East against alien interests. But Japan has not taken long to betray that rising hope and repudiate all that seemed significant in her wonderful, and, to us symbolic, awakening, and has now become itself a worse menace to the defenceless peoples of the East. How to view Japan's position in the Second World War was a divisive issue in India.

After the war, when Japanese political leaders were tried for war crimes, the sole dissenting voice among the judges came from the Indian judge, Radhabinod Pal, a distinguished jurist. Pal dissented on various grounds, among them that no fair trial was possible in view of the asymmetry of power between the victor and the defeated. Ambivalent feelings in India toward the Japanese military aggression, given the unacceptable nature of British imperialism, possibly had a part in predisposing Pal to consider a perspective different from that of the other judges.

More tellingly, Subhas Chandra Bose (no relation of Rash Behari Bose), a leading nationalist, made his way to Japan during the war via Italy and Germany after escaping from a British prison; he helped the Japanese to form units of Indian soldiers, who had earlier surrendered to the advancing Japanese army, to fight on the Japanese side as the "Indian National Army." Rabindranath had formerly entertained great admiration for Subhas Bose as a dedicated nonsectarian fighter for Indian independence. But their ways would have parted when Bose's political activities took this turn, although Tagore was dead by the time Bose reached Japan.

Tagore saw Japanese militarism as illustrating the way nationalism can mislead even a nation of great achievement and promise. In 1938 Yone Noguchi, the distinguished poet and friend of Tagore (as well as of Yeats and Pound), wrote to Tagore, pleading with him to change his mind about Japan. Rabindranath's reply, written on September 12, 1938, was altogether uncompromising:

It seems to me that it is futile for either of us to try to

convince the other, since your faith in the infallible right of Japan to bully other Asiatic nations into line with your Government's policy is not shared by me.... Believe me, it is sorrow and shame, not anger, that prompt me to write to you. I suffer intensely not only because the reports of Chinese suffering batter against my heart, but because I can no longer point out with pride the example of a great Japan.

He would have been much happier with the postwar emergence of Japan as a peaceful power. Then, too, since he was not free of egotism, he would also have been pleased by the attention paid to his ideas by the novelist Yasunari Kawabata and others.

International Concerns: Tagore was not invariably well-informed about international politics. He allowed himself to be entertained by Mussolini in a short visit to Italy in May-June 1926, a visit arranged by Carlo Formichi, professor of Sanskrit at the University of Rome. When he asked to meet Benedetto Croce, Formichi said, "Impossible! Impossible!" Mussolini told him that Croce was "not in Rome." When Tagore said he would go "wherever he is," Mussolini assured him that Croce's whereabouts were unknown.

Such incidents, as well as warnings from Romain Rolland and other friends, should have ended Tagore's flirtation with Mussolini more quickly than it did. But only after he received graphic accounts of the brutality of Italian fascism from two exiles, Gaetano Salvemini and Gaetano Salvadori, and learned more of what was happening in Italy, did he publicly denounce the regime, publishing a letter to the *Manchester Guardian* in August. The next month, Popolo d'Italia, the magazine edited by Benito Mussolini's brother, replied: "Who cares? Italy laughs at Tagore and those who brought this unctuous and insupportable fellow in our midst."

With his high expectations of Britain, Tagore continued to be surprised by what he took to be a lack of official sympathy for international victims of aggression. He returned to this theme in the lecture he gave on his last birthday, in 1941: While Japan was quietly devouring North China, her act of wanton aggression was ignored as a minor incident by the veterans of British diplomacy. We have also witnessed from this distance how actively the British statesmen acquiesced in the destruction of the Spanish Republic. But distinguishing between the British government and the British people, Rabindranath went on to note "with admiration how a band of valiant Englishmen laid down their lives for Spain."

Tagore's view of the Soviet Union has been a subject of much discussion. He was widely read in Russia. In 1917 several Russian translations of *Gitanjali* (one edited by Ivan Bunin, later the first Russian Nobel Laureate in Literature) were available, and by the late 1920s many of the English versions of his work had been rendered into Russian by several distinguished translators. Russian versions of his work continued to appear: Boris Pasternak translated him in the 1950s and 1960s.

When Tagore visited Russia in 1930, he was much impressed by its development efforts and by what he saw as a real commitment to eliminate poverty and economic inequality. But what impressed him most was the expansion of basic education across the old Russian empire. In Letters from Russia, written in Bengali and published in 1931, he unfavorably compares the acceptance of widespread illiteracy in India by the British administration with Russian efforts to expand education:

In stepping on the soil of Russia, the first thing that caught my eye was that in education, at any rate, the peasant and the working classes have made such enormous progress in these few years that nothing comparable has happened even to our highest classes in the course of the last hundred and fifty years.... The people here are not at all afraid of giving complete education even to Turcomans of distant Asia; on the contrary, they are utterly in earnest about it.

When parts of the book were translated into English in 1934, the under-secretary for India stated in Parliament that it was "calculated by distortion of the facts to bring the British Administration in India into contempt and disrepute," and the book was then promptly banned. The English version would not be published until after independence.

Education and Freedom: The British Indian administrators

were not, however, alone in trying to suppress Tagore's reflections on Russia. They were joined by Soviet officials. In an interview with *Izvestia* in 1930, Tagore sharply criticized the lack of freedom that he observed in Russia:

I must ask you: Are you doing your ideal a service by arousing in the minds of those under your training anger, class-hatred, and revengefulness against those whom you consider to be your enemies?... Freedom of mind is needed for the reception of truth; terror hopelessly kills it.... For the sake of humanity I hope you may never create a vicious force of violence, which will go on weaving an interminable chain of violence and cruelty.... You have tried to destroy many of the other evils of [the czarist] period. Why not try to destroy this one also? The interview was not published in *Izvestia* until 1988—nearly sixty years later. Tagore's reaction to the Russia of 1930 arose from two of his strongest commitments: his uncompromising belief in the importance of "freedom of mind" (the source of his criticism of the Soviet Union), and his conviction that the expansion of basic education is central to social progress (the source of his praise, particularly in contrast to British-run India). He identified the lack of basic education as the fundamental cause of many of India's social and economic afflictions:

In my view the imposing tower of misery which today rests on the heart of India has its sole foundation in the absence of education. Caste divisions, religious conflicts, aversion to work, precarious economic conditions - all centre on this single factor. It was on education (and on the reflection, dialogue, and communication that are associated with it), rather than on, say, spinning "as a sacrifice" ("the charka does not require anyone to think"), that the future of India would depend.

Tagore was concerned not only that there be wider opportunities for education across the country (especially in rural areas where schools were few), but also that the schools themselves be more lively and enjoyable. He himself had dropped out of school early, largely out of boredom, and had never bothered to earn a diploma. He wrote extensively on how schools should be made more attractive to boys and girls and thus more productive. His own co-educational school at Santiniketan had many progressive features. The emphasis here was on self-motivation rather than on discipline, and on fostering intellectual curiosity rather than competitive excellence. Much of Rabindranath's life was spent in developing the school at Santiniketan. The school never had much money, since the fees were very low. His lecture honoraria, "$700 a scold," went to support it, as well as most of his Nobel Prize money. The school received no support from the government, but did get help from private citizens—even Mahatma Gandhi raised money for it.

The dispute with Mahatma Gandhi on the Bihar earthquake touched on a subject that was very important to Tagore: the need for education in science as well as in literature and the humanities. At Santiniketan, there were strong "local" elements in its emphasis on Indian traditions, including the classics, and in the use of Bengali rather than English as the language of instruction. At the same time there were courses on a great variety of cultures, and study programs devoted to China, Japan, and the Middle East. Many foreigners came to Santiniketan to study or teach, and the fusion of studies seemed to work.

I am partial to seeing Tagore as an educator, having myself been educated at Santiniketan. The school was unusual in many different ways, such as the oddity that classes, excepting those requiring a laboratory, were held outdoors (whenever the weather permitted). No matter what we thought of Rabindranath's belief that one gains from being in a natural setting while learning (some of us argued about this theory), we typically found the experience of outdoor schooling extremely attractive and pleasant.

Academically, our school was not particularly exacting (often we did not have any examinations at all), and it could not, by the usual academic standards, compete with some of the better schools in Calcutta. But there was something remarkable about the ease with which class discussions could move from Indian traditional literature to contemporary as well as classical Western thought, and then to the culture of

China or Japan or elsewhere. The school's celebration of variety was also in sharp contrast with the cultural conservatism and separatism that has tended to grip India from time to time. The cultural give and take of Tagore's vision of the contemporary world has close parallels with the vision of Satyajit Ray, also an alumnus of Santiniketan who made several films based on Tagore's stories. Ray's words about Santiniketan in 1991 would have greatly pleased Rabindranath:

I consider the three years I spent in Santiniketan as the most fruitful of my life.... Santiniketan opened my eyes for the first time to the splendours of Indian and Far Eastern art. Until then I was completely under the sway of Western art, music and literature. Santiniketan made me the combined product of East and West that I am.

India Today: At the fiftieth anniversary of Indian independence, the reckoning of what India had or had not achieved in this half century was a subject of considerable interest: "What has been the story of those first fifty years?" (as Shashi Tharoor asked in his balanced, informative, and highly readable account of *India: From Midnight to the Millennium*).

If Tagore were to see the India of today, more than half a century after independence, nothing perhaps would shock him so much as the continued illiteracy of the masses. He would see this as a total betrayal of what the nationalist leaders had promised during the struggle for independence—a promise that had figured even in Nehru's rousing speech on the eve of independence in August 1947 (on India's "tryst with destiny").

In view of his interest in childhood education, Tagore would not be consoled by the extraordinary expansion of university education, in which India sends to its universities six times as many people per unit of population as does China. Rather, he would be stunned that, in contrast to East and Southeast Asia, including China, half the adult population and two thirds of Indian women remain unable to read or write. Statistically reliable surveys indicate that even in the late 1980s, nearly half of the rural girls between the ages of twelve and fourteen did not attend any school for a single day of their lives. This state of affairs is the result of the continuation of British imperial neglect of mass education, which has been reinforced by India's traditional elitism, as well as upper-class-dominated contemporary politics (except in parts of India such as Kerala, where anti-upper-caste movements have tended to concentrate on education as a great leveller). Tagore would see illiteracy and the neglect of education not only as the main source of India's continued social backwardness, but also as a great constraint that restricts the possibility and reach of economic development in India (as his writings on rural development forcefully make clear). Tagore would also have strongly felt the need for a greater commitment—and a greater sense of urgency—in removing endemic poverty.

At the same time, Tagore would undoubtedly find some satisfaction in the survival of democracy in India, in its relatively free press, and in general from the "freedom of mind" that post-independence Indian politics has, on the whole, managed to maintain. He would also be pleased by the fact noted by the historian E.P. Thompson (whose father Edward Thompson had written one of the first major biographies of Tagore:

All the convergent influences of the world run through this society: Hindu, Moslem, Christian, secular; Stalinist, liberal, Maoist, democratic socialist, Gandhian. There is not a thought that is being thought in the West or East that is not active in some Indian mind.

Tagore would have been happy also to see that the one governmental attempt to dispense generally with basic liberties and political and civil rights in India, in the 1970s, when Prime Minister Indira Gandhi (ironically, herself a former student at Santiniketan) declared an "emergency," was overwhelmingly rejected by the Indian voters, leading to the precipitate fall of her government.

Rabindranath would also see that the changes in policy that have eliminated famine since independence had much to do with the freedom to be heard in a democratic India. In Tagore's play *Raja O Rani* ("The King and the Queen"), the sympathetic Queen eventually rebels against the callousness of state policy toward the hungry. She begins by inquiring about the ugly sounds outside the palace, only to be told that the noise is coming from "the coarse, clamorous crowd who howl unashamedly for food and disturb the sweet peace of the palace." The Viceregal office in India could have taken a similarly callous view of Indian famines, right up to the easily preventable Bengal famine of 1943, just before independence, which killed between two and three million people. But a government in a multi-party democracy, with elections and free newspapers, cannot any longer dismiss the noise from "the coarse, clamorous crowd."

Unlike Gandhi, Rabindranath would not resent the development of modern industries in India, or the acceleration of technical progress, since he did not want India to be shackled to the turning of "the wheel of an antiquated invention." Tagore was concerned that people not be dominated by machines, but he was not opposed to making good use of modern technology. "The mastery over the machine," he wrote in *Crisis in Civilization,* "by which the British have consolidated their sovereignty over their vast empire, has been kept a sealed book, to which due access has been denied to this helpless country." Rabindranath had a deep interest in the environment - he was particularly concerned about deforestation and initiated a "festival of tree-planting" (vriksha-ropana) as early as 1928. He would want increased private and government commitments to environmentalism; but he would not derive from this position a general case against modern industry and technology.

On Cultural Separation: Rabindranath would be shocked by the growth of cultural separatism in India, as elsewhere. The "openness" that he valued so much is certainly under great strain right now - in many countries. Religious fundamentalism still has a relatively small following in India; but various factions seem to be doing their best to increase their numbers. Certainly religious sectarianism has had much success in some parts of India (particularly in the west and the north). Tagore would see the expansion of religious sectarianism as being closely associated with an artificially separatist view of culture. He would have strongly resisted defining India in specifically Hindu terms, rather than as a "confluence" of many cultures. Even after the partition of 1947, India is still the third- largest Muslim country in the world, with more Muslims than in Bangladesh, and nearly as many as in Pakistan. Only Indonesia has substantially more followers of Islam. Indeed, by pointing to the immense heterogeneousness of India's cultural background and its richly diverse history, Tagore had argued that the "idea of India" itself militated against a culturally separatist view—"against the intense consciousness of the separateness of one's own people from others."

Tagore would also oppose the cultural nationalism that has recently been gaining some ground in India, along with an exaggerated fear of the influence of the West. He was uncompromising in his belief that human beings could absorb quite different cultures in constructive ways:

Whatever we understand and enjoy in human products instantly becomes ours, wherever they might have their origin. I am proud of my humanity when I can acknowledge the poets and artists of other countries as my own. Let me feel with unalloyed gladness that all the great glories of man are mine. Therefore it hurts me deeply when the cry of rejection rings loud against the West in my country with the clamour that Western education can only injure us.

In this context, it is important to emphasize that Rabindranath was not short of pride in India's own heritage, and often spoke about it. He lectured at Oxford, with evident satisfaction, on the importance of India's religious ideas—quoting both from ancient texts and from popular poetry (such as the verses of the sixteenth-century Muslim poet Kabir). In 1940, when he was given an honorary doctorate by Oxford University, in a ceremony arranged at his own educational establishment in Santiniketan ("In Gangem Defluit Isis," Oxford helpfully explained), to the predictable "volley of Latin" Tagore responded "by a volley of Sanskrit," as Marjorie Sykes, a Quaker friend of Rabindranath, reports. Her cheerful summary of the match, "India held its own," was not out of line with Tagore's pride in Indian culture. His welcoming attitude to Western civilization was reinforced by this confidence: he did not see India's culture as fragile and in need of "protection" from Western influence.

In India, he wrote, "circumstances almost compel us to learn English, and this lucky accident has given us the opportunity of access into the richest of all poetical literatures of the world." There seems to me much force in Rabindranath's argument for clearly distinguishing between the injustice of a serious asymmetry of power (colonialism being a prime example of this) and the importance nevertheless of appraising Western culture in an open-minded way, in colonial and postcolonial territories, in order to see what uses could be made of it.

Rabindranath insisted on open debate on every issue, and distrusted conclusions based on a mechanical formula, no matter how attractive that formula might seem in isolation (such as "This was forced on us by our colonial masters - we must reject it," "This is our tradition—we must follow it," "We have promised to do this—we must fulfill that promise," and so on). The question he persistently asks is whether we have reason enough to want what is being proposed, taking everything into account. Important as history is, reasoning has to go beyond the past. It is in the sovereignty of reasoning—fearless reasoning in freedom—that we can find Rabindranath Tagore's lasting voice.

Chapter 3

Works

Tagore's Bengali-language initials are worked into this "Ra-Tha" wooden seal, which bears close stylistic similarity to designs used in traditional Haida carvings. Tagore often embellished his manuscripts with such art.

Tagore's literary reputation is disproportionately influenced by regard for his poetry; however, he also wrote novels, essays, short stories, travelogues, dramas, and thousands of songs. Of Tagore's prose, his short stories are perhaps most highly regarded; indeed, he is credited with originating the Bengali-language version of the genre. His works are frequently noted for their rhythmic, optimistic, and lyrical nature. Such stories mostly borrow from deceptively simple subject matter: the lives of ordinary people.

Novels and Non-fiction

Tagore wrote eight novels and four novellas, including *Chaturanga*, *Shesher Kobita*, *Char Odhay*, and *Noukadubi*. *Ghare Baire* (*The Home and the World*)—through the lens of the idealistic *zamindar* protagonist Nikhil—excoriates rising Indian nationalism, terrorism, and religious zeal in the *Swadeshi* movement; a frank expression of Tagore's conflicted sentiments, it emerged out of a 1914 bout of depression. Indeed, the novel bleakly ends with Hindu-Muslim sectarian violence and Nikhil's being (probably mortally) wounded.

In some sense, *Gora* shares the same theme, raising controversial questions regarding the Indian identity. As with *Ghore Baire*, matters of self-identity (*jti*), personal freedom, and religion are developed in the context of a family story and love triangle. Another powerful story is *Jogajog* (*Relationships*), where the heroine Kumudini—bound by the ideals of *Shiva-Sati*, exemplified by Dkshyani—is torn between her pity for the sinking fortunes of her progressive and compassionate elder brother and his foil: her exploitative, rakish, and patriarchical husband. In it, Tagore demonstrates his feminist leanings, using *pathos* to depict the plight and ultimate demise of Bengali women trapped by pregnancy, duty, and family honour; simultaneously, he treats the decline of Bengal's landed oligarchy.

Other novels were more uplifting: *Shesher Kobita* (translated twice—*Last Poem* and *Farewell Song*) is his most lyrical novel, with poems and rhythmic passages written by the main character (a poet). It also contains elements of satire and postmodernism; stock characters gleefully attack the reputation of an old, outmoded, oppressively renowned poet who, incidentally, goes by the name of Rabindranath Tagore. Though his novels remain among the least-appreciated of his works, they have been given renewed attention via film adaptations by such directors as Satyajit Ray; these include *Chokher Bali* and *Ghare Baire*; many have soundtracks featuring selections from Tagore's own *rabindrasangit*. Tagore wrote many non-fiction books, writing on topics ranging from Indian history to linguistics. Aside from autobiographical works, his travelogues, essays, and lectures were compiled into several volumes, including *Iurop Jatrir Patro* (*Letters from Europe*) and *Manusher Dhormo* (*The Religion of Man*).

Music and Artwork

Tagore was a prolific musician and painter, writing around 2,230 songs. They comprise *rabindrasangit*, now an integral part of Bengali culture. Tagore's music is inseparable from his literature, most of which—poems or parts of novels, stories, or plays alike—became lyrics for his songs. Primarily influenced by the *thumri* style of Hindustani classical music, they ran the entire gamut of human emotion, ranging from his early dirge-like Brahmo devotional hymns to quasi-erotic compositions. They emulated the tonal colour of classical *ragas* to varying extents. Though at times his songs mimicked a given raga's melody and rhythm faithfully, he also blended elements of different ragas to create innovative works.

For Bengalis, their appeal, stemming from the combination of emotive strength and beauty described as surpassing even Tagore's poetry, was such that the *Modern Review* observed that "[t]here is in Bengal no cultured home where Rabindranath's songs are not sung or at least attempted to be sung... Even illiterate villagers sing his songs". Music critic Arthur Strangways of *The Observer* first introduced non-Bengalis to *rabindrasangeet* with his book *The Music of Hindostan,* which described it as a "vehicle of a personality... [that] go behind this or that system of music to that beauty of sound which all systems put out their hands to seize."

Among them are Bangladesh's national anthem *Amar Shonar Bangla* ; Tagore thus became the only person ever to have written the national anthems of two nations. In turn, *rabindrasangeet* influenced the styles of such musicians as sitar maestro Vilayat Khan, and the *sarodiyas* Buddhadev Dasgupta and Amjad Ali Khan. Much of Tagore's artwork dabbled in primitivism, including this pastel-coloured rendition of a Malanggan mask from northern New Ireland. At age sixty, Tagore took up drawing and painting; successful exhibitions of his many works—which made a debut appearance in Paris upon encouragement by artists he met in the south of France—were held throughout Europe.

Tagore—who likely exhibited protanopia ("colour blindness"), or partial lack of (red-green, in Tagore's case) colour discernment—painted in a style characterised by peculiarities in aesthetics and colouring schemes. Nevertheless, Tagore took to emulating numerous styles, including that of craftwork by the Malanggan people of northern New Ireland, Haida carvings from the west coast of Canada (British Columbia), and woodcuts by Max Pechstein. Tagore also had an artist's eye for his own handwriting, embellishing the scribbles, cross-outs, and word layouts in his manuscripts with simple artistic leitmotifs, including simple rhythmic designs.

Theatrical Pieces

Tagore's experience in theatre began at age sixteen, when he played the lead role in his brother Jyotirindranath's adaptation of Molière's *Le Bourgeois Gentilhomme*. At age twenty, he wrote his first drama-opera—*Valmiki Pratibha* (*The Genius of Valmiki*)—which describes how the bandit Valmiki reforms his ethos, is blessed by Saraswati, and composes the *Râmâyana*. Through it, Tagore vigorously explores a wide range of dramatic styles and emotions, including usage of revamped *kirtans* and adaptation of traditional English and Irish folk melodies as drinking songs.

Another notable play, *Dak Ghar* (*The Post Office*), describes how a child—striving to escape his stuffy confines—ultimately "fall[s] asleep" (which suggests his physical death). A story with worldwide appeal (it received rave reviews in Europe), *Dak Ghar* dealt with death as, in Tagore's words, "spiritual freedom" from "the world of hoarded wealth and certified creeds". His other works—emphasizing fusion of lyrical flow and emotional rhythm tightly focused on a core idea—were unlike previous Bengali dramas.

His works sought to articulate, in Tagore's words, "the play of feeling and not of action". In 1890 he wrote *Visarjan* (*Sacrifice*), regarded as his finest drama. The Bengali-language originals included intricate subplots and extended monologues. Later, his dramas probed more philosophical and allegorical themes; these included *Dak Ghar*. Another is Tagore's *Chandalika* (*Untouchable Girl*), which was modeled on an ancient Buddhist legend describing how Ananda—the Gautama Buddha's disciple—asks water of an *Adivasi* ("untouchable") girl.

Lastly, among his most famous dramas is *Raktakaravi* (*Red Oleanders*), which tells of a kleptocratic king who enriches himself by forcing his subjects to mine. The heroine, Nandini, eventually rallies the common people to destroy these symbols of subjugation. Tagore's other plays include *Chitrangada, Raja,* and *Mayar Khela.* Dance dramas based on Tagore's plays are commonly referred to as *rabindra nritya natyas.*

Short Stories

A drawing by Nandalall Bose illustrating Tagore's short story "The Hero", an English-language translation of which appeared in the 1913 Macmillan publication of Tagore's *The Crescent Moon.*

Tagore's "Sadhana" period, comprising the four years from 1891 to 1895, was named for one of Tagore's magazines. This period was among Tagore 's most fecund, yielding more than half the stories contained in the three-volume *Galpaguchchha,* which itself is a collection of eighty-four stories. Such stories usually showcase Tagore's reflections upon his surroundings, on modern and fashionable ideas, and on interesting mind puzzles (which Tagore was fond of testing his intellect with).

Tagore typically associated his earliest stories (such as those of the "*Sadhana*" period) with an exuberance of vitality and spontaneity; these characteristics were intimately connected with Tagore's life in the common villages of, among others, Patisar, Shajadpur, and Shilaida while managing the Tagore family's vast landholdings. There, he beheld the lives of India's poor and common people; Tagore thereby took to examining their lives with a penetrative depth and feeling that was singular in Indian literature up to that point.

In "The Fruitseller from Kabul", Tagore speaks in first person as town-dweller and novelist who chances upon the Afghani seller. He attempts to distil the sense of longing felt by those long trapped in the mundane and hardscrabble confines of Indian urban life, giving play to dreams of a different existence in the distant and wild mountains: "There were autumn mornings, the time of year when kings of old went forth to conquest; and I, never stirring from my little corner in Calcutta, would let my mind wander over the whole world. At the very name of another country, my heart would go out to it... I would fall to weaving a network of dreams: the mountains, the glens, the forest.... ". Many of the other *Galpaguchchha* stories were written in Tagore's *Sabuj Patra* period (1914–1917; also named for one of Tagore's magazines).

A 1913 illustration by Asit Kumar Haldar accompanying

"The Beginning", a prose-poem appearing in Tagore's *The Crescent Moon.* Tagore's *Golpoguchchho* (*Bunch of Stories*) remains among Bengali literature's most popular fictional works, providing subject matter for many successful films and theatrical plays. Satyajit Ray's film *Charulata* was based upon Tagore's controversial novella, *Nastanirh* (*The Broken Nest*). In *Atithi* (also made into a film), the young Brahmin boy Tarapada shares a boat ride with a village zamindar.

The boy reveals that he has run away from home, only to wander around ever since. Taking pity, the zamindar adopts him and ultimately arranges his marriage to the zamindar's own daughter. However, the night before the wedding, Tarapada runs off—again. *Strir Patra* (*The Letter from the Wife*) is among Bengali literature's earliest depictions of the bold emancipation of women.

The heroine Mrinal, the wife of a typical patriarchical Bengali middle class man, writes a letter while she is traveling (which constitutes the whole story). It details the pettiness of her life and struggles; she finally declares that she will not return to her husband's home with the statement *Amio bachbo. Ei bachlum* ("And I shall live. Here, I live"). In *Haimanti,* Tagore takes on the institution of Hindu marriage, describing the dismal lifelessness of married Bengali women, hypocrisies plaguing the Indian middle classes, and how Haimanti, a sensitive young woman, must—due to her sensitiveness and free spirit—sacrifice her life.

In the last passage, Tagore directly attacks the Hindu custom of glorifying Sita's attempted self-immolation as a means of appeasing her husband Rama's doubts. Tagore also examines Hindu-Muslim tensions in *Musalmani Didi,* which in many ways embodies the essence of Tagore's humanism. On the other hand, *Darpaharan* exhibits Tagore's self-consciousness, describing a young man harboring literary ambitions.

Though he loves his wife, he wishes to stifle her own literary career, deeming it unfeminine. Tagore himself, in his youth, seems to have harbored similar ideas about women. *Darpaharan* depicts the final humbling of the man via his acceptance of his wife's talents. As many other Tagore stories, *Jibito o Mrito* provides the Bengalis with one of their more widely used epigrams: *Kadombini moriya proman korilo she more nai* ("Kadombini died, thereby proved that she hadn't").

Poetry

Tagore's poetry—which varied in style from classical formalism to the comic, visionary, and ecstatic—proceeds out a lineage established by 15th- and 16th-century VaicGava poets. Tagore was also influenced by the mysticism of the *rishi*-authors who—including Vyasa—wrote the Upanishads, the Bhakta-Sufi mystic Kabir, and Ramprasad.[65] Yet Tagore's poetry became most innovative and mature after his exposure to rural Bengal's folk music, which included ballads sung by Bul folk singers—especially the bard Llan Zh.[66][67] These—which were rediscovered and popularised by Tagore—resemble 19th-century Kartbhaj hymns that emphasize inward divinity and rebellion against religious and social orthodoxy.

During his Shilaidaha years, his poems took on a lyrical quality, speaking via the *maner manus* (the Bâuls' "man within the heart") or meditating upon the *jivan devata* ("living God within"). This figure thus sought connection with divinity through appeal to nature and the emotional interplay of human drama. Tagore used such techniques in his BhnusiCha poems (which chronicle the romance between Radha and Krishna), which he repeatedly revised over the course of seventy years. Later, Tagore responded to the (mostly) crude emergence of modernism and realism in Bengali literature by writing experimental works in the 1930s. Examples works include *Africa* and *Camalia,* which are among the better known of his latter poems. He also occasionally wrote poems using *Shadhu Bhasha* (a Sanskritised dialect of Bengali); later, he began using *Cholti Bhasha* (a more popular dialect). Other notable works include *Manasi, Sonar Tori* (*Golden Boat*), *Balaka* (*Wild Geese*—the title being a metaphor for migrating souls), and *Purobi. Sonar Tori*'s most famous poem—dealing with the ephemeral nature of life and achievement—goes by the same name; it ends with the haunting phrase "

Key ideas

Rabindranath did not write a central educational treatise, and his ideas must be gleaned through his various writings and educational experiments at Santiniketan In general, he envisioned an education that was deeply rooted in one's immediate surroundings but connected to the cultures of the wider world, predicated upon pleasurable learning and individualized to the personality of the child. He felt that a curriculum should revolve organically around nature with classes held in the open air under the trees to provide for a spontaneous appreciation of the fluidity of the plant and animal kingdoms, and seasonal changes.

Children sat on hand-woven mats beneath the trees, which they were allowed to climb and run beneath between classes. Nature walks and excursions were a part of the curriculum and students were encouraged to follow the life cycles of insects, birds and plants. Class schedules were made flexible to allow for shifts in the weather or special attention to natural phenomena, and seasonal festivals were created for the children by Tagore. In an essay entitled "A Poet's School," he emphasizes the importance of an empathetic sense of interconnectedness with the surrounding world:

We have come to this world to accept it, not merely to know it. We may become powerful by knowledge, but we attain fullness by sympathy. The highest education is that which does not merely give us information but makes our life in harmony with all existence. But we find that this education of sympathy is not only systematically ignored in schools, but it is severely repressed. From our very childhood habits are formed and knowledge is imparted in such a manner that our life is weaned away from nature and our mind and the world are set in opposition from the beginning of our days.

Thus the greatest of educations for which we came prepared is neglected, and we are made to lose our world to find a bagful of information instead. We rob the child of his earth to teach him geography, of language to teach him grammar. His hunger is for the Epic, but he is supplied with chronicles of facts and dates...Child-nature protests against such calamity with all its power of suffering, subdued at last into silence by punishment. In Tagore's philosophy of education, the aesthetic development of the senses was as important as the intellectual—if not more so—and music, literature, art, dance and drama were given great prominence in the daily life of the school. This was particularly so after the first decade of the school.

Drawing on his home life at Jorasanko, Rabindranath tried to create an atmosphere in which the arts would become instinctive. One of the first areas to be emphasized was music. Rabindranath writes that in his adolescence, a 'cascade of musical emotion' gushed forth day after day at Jorasanko. 'We felt we would try to test everything,' he writes, 'and no achievement seemed impossible...We wrote, we sang, we acted, we poured ourselves out on every side.

In keeping with his theory of subconscious learning, Rabindranath never talked or wrote down to the students, but rather involved them with whatever he was writing or composing. The students were allowed access to the room where he read his new writings to teachers and critics, and they were encouraged to read out their own writings in special literary evenings. In teaching also he believed in presenting difficult levels of literature, which the students might not fully grasp, but which would stimulate them. The writing and publishing of periodicals had always been an important aspect of Jorasanko life, and students at Santiniketan were encouraged to create their own publications and put out several illustrated magazines. The children were encouraged to follow their ideas in painting and drawing and to draw inspiration from the many visiting artists and writers.

Most of Rabindranath's dramas were written at Santiniketan and the students took part in both the performing and production sides. He writes how well the students were able to enter into the spirit of the dramas and perform their roles, which required subtle understanding and sympathy without special training. As Rabindranath began conceiving of Visva-Bharati as a national centre for the arts, he encouraged artists such as Nandalal Bose to take up residence at

Santiniketan and to devote themselves full-time to promoting a national form of art. Without music and the fine arts, he wrote, a nation lacks its highest means of national self-expression and the people remain inarticulate. Tagore was one of the first to support and bring together different forms of Indian dance. He helped revive folk dances and introduced dance forms from other parts of India, such as Manipuri, Kathak and Kathakali. He also supported modern dance and was one of the first to recognize the talents of Uday Sankar, who was invited to perform at Santiniketan.

The meeting-ground of cultures, as Rabindranath envisioned it at Visva-Bharati, should be a learning centre where conflicting interests are minimized, where individuals work together in a common pursuit of truth and realise 'that artists in all parts of the world have created forms of beauty, scientists discovered secrets of the universe, philosophers solved the problems of existence, saints made the truth of the spiritual world organic in their own lives, not merely for some particular race to which they belonged, but for all mankind.'

To encourage mutuality, Rabindranath invited artists and scholars from other parts of India and the world to live together at Santiniketan on a daily basis to share their cultures with Visva-Bharati. The Constitution designated Visva-Bharati as an Indian, Eastern and Global cultural centre whose goals were:

- To study the mind of Man in its realisation of different aspects of truth from diverse points of view.
- To bring into more intimate relation with one another through patient study and research, the different cultures of the East on the basis of their underlying unity.
- To approach the West from the standpoint of such a unity of the life and thought of Asia.
- To seek to realise in a common fellowship of study the meeting of East and West and thus ultimately to strengthen the fundamental conditions of world peace through the free communication of ideas between the two hemispheres.

- And with such Ideals in view to provide at Santiniketan a centre of culture where research into the study of the religion, literature, history, science and art of Hindu, Buddhist, Jain, Zoroastrian, Islamic, Sikh, Christian and other civilizations may be pursued along with the culture of the West, with that simplicity of externals which is necessary for true spiritual realisation, in amity, good-fellowship and co-operation between the thinkers and scholars of both Eastern and Western countries, free from all antagonisms of race, nationality, creed or caste and in the name of the One Supreme Being who is Shantam, Shivam, Advaitam.

In terms of curriculum, he advocated a different emphasis in teaching. Rather than studying national cultures for the wars won and cultural dominance imposed, he advocated a teaching system that analysed history and culture for the progress that had been made in breaking down social and religious barriers. Such an approach emphasized the innovations that had been made in integrating individuals of diverse backgrounds into a larger framework, and in devising the economic policies which emphasized social justice and narrowed the gap between rich and poor. Art would be studied for its role in furthering the aesthetic imagination and expressing universal themes.

It should be noted that Rabindranath in his own person was a living icon of the type of mutuality and creative exchange that he advocated. His vision of culture was not a static one, but one that advocated new cultural fusions, and he fought for a world where multiple voices were encouraged to interact with one another and to reconcile differences within an overriding commitment to peace and mutual interconnectedness. His generous personality and his striving to break down barriers of all sorts gives us a model for the way multiculturalism can exist within a single human personality, and the type of individual which the educational process should be aspiring towards.

Tagore's educational efforts were ground-breaking in

many areas. He was one of the first in India to argue for a humane educational system that was in touch with the environment and aimed at overall development of the personality. Santiniketan became a model for vernacular instruction and the development of Bengali textbooks; as well, it offered one of the earliest coeducational programs in South Asia. The establishment of Visva-Bharati and Sriniketan led to pioneering efforts in many directions, including models for distinctively Indian higher education and mass education, as well as pan-Asian and global cultural exchange.

One characteristic that sets Rabindranath's educational theory apart is his approach to education as a poet. At Santiniketan, he stated, his goal was to create a poem 'in a medium other than words.' It was this poetic vision that enabled him to fashion a scheme of education which was all inclusive, and to devise a unique programme for education in nature and creative self-expression in a learning climate congenial to global cultural exchange.

Conclusion

Rabindranath Tagore, by his efforts and achievements, is part of a global network of pioneering educators, such as Rousseau, Pestalozzi, Froebel, Montessori and Dewey—and in the contemporary context, Malcolm Knowles—who have striven to create non-authoritarian learning systems appropriate to their respective surroundings. In a poem that expresses Tagore's goals for international education, he writes:

Where the mind is without fear and the head is held high,

Where knowledge is free;

Where the world has not been broken up into fragments by narrow domestic walls;

Where words come out from the depth of truth;

Where tireless striving stretches its arms towards perfection;

Where the clear stream of reason has not lost its way into the dreary desert sand of dead habit; Where the mind is led forward by thee into ever-widening thought and action– into that heaven of freedom, my Father, Let my country awake

Tagore's literary life extened over sixty years, and he reminds one of Victor Hugo in the copiousness and variety of his work: over one thousand poems; nearly two dozen plays and playlets; eight novels; eightor more volumes of short stories; more than two thousands songs, of which he wrote both the words and the music; and a mass of prose on literary, social, religious, political, and other topics. Add to these his english translations; his paintings; his travels and lecture-tours in Asia, America, and Europe; and his activities as educationist, as social and religious reformer, and as politician- and there you have, judged by quantity alone, the life-work of a Titan. Thia is not to say that his genius was no more than the capacity for taking infinite pains; but to note the element of steel and concrete that went to his making, and thus to dispose of the legend, that has grown in some quarters in recent years, of Tagore the pale-lily poet of ladies' table.

Not that the legend is entirely baseless. Tagore's almost continuous iteration, in his English translations, of the softer side of his poetry and his wistful-mystical message, is partly responsible for it. After having won world-fame with the mystical-devotional poetry of the English Gitanjali, he dug overmuch along that particular seam, producing a monotonously one-sided impression of his work. It is true that *The Gardener* and the subsequent volumes of translations gave some of his best lyrics, but they also gave many poems which were very thin and had nothing beyond a delicate fancy or a pretty sensibility to show for their author

Selected works

- Kabikahini, 1878 - a poet's tale
- Sadhya sangeet, 1882 - evening songs
- Prabhat sangeet, 1883 - morning songs
- Bau-thakuranir hat, 1883
- Rajashi, 1887
- Raja o rani, 1889 - the king and the queen/devouring love
- Visargan, 1890 - sacrifice
- Manasi, 1890

- Iurope-jatrir diari, 1891, 1893
- Valmiki pratibha, 1893
- Sonar tari, 1894 - the golden boat
- Khanika, 1900 - moments
- Katha, 1900
- Kalpana, 1900
- Naivedya, 1901
- Nashtanir, 1901 - the broken nest
- Sharan, 1902
- Binodini, 1902
- Chocher bali, 1903 - eyesore
- Naukadubi, 1905 - haaksirikko
- Kheya, 1906
- Naukadubi, 1906 - the wreck
- Gora, 1907-09 - suom.
- Saradotsava, 1908 - autumn festival
- Galpaguccha, 1912 - a bunch of stories
- Chinnapatra, 1912
- Viday-abhisap, 1912 - the curse at farewell
- Gitanjali, 1912 - song offerings (new translation in 2000 by joen winter, publ. Anvil press) - uhrilauluja
- Jiban smrti, 1912 - my reminiscenes - elämäni muistoja, trans. By j. Hollo
- Dakghar, 1912 - post office
- The crescent moon, 1913
- Glimpses of bengal life, 1913
- The hungry stones and other stories, 1913
- Chitra, 1914 - transl.
- Ghitimalaya, 1914
- The king of the dark chamber, 1914
- The post office, 1914
- Sadhana, 1914
- Ghare-baire, 1916 - the home and the world - koti ja maailma
- Balak, 1916 - a flight of swans
- Chaturanga, 1916 - transl.
- Fruit gathering, 1916
- The hungry stones, 1916

- Stray birds, 1916
- Personality, 1917 - persoonallisuus
- The cycle of spring, 1917
- Sacrifice, and other plays, 1917
- My reminiscene, 1917
- Nationalism, 1917
- Mashi and other stories, 1918
- Stories from tagore, 1918
- Palataka, 1918
- Japan-jatri, 1919 - a visit to japan
- Greater india, 1921
- The fugitive, 1921
- Creative unity, 1921
- Lipika, 1922
- Muktadhara, 1922 - trans.
- Poems, 1923
- Gora, 1924
- Letters from abroad, 1924
- Red oleander, 1924
- Grihaprabesh, 1925
- Broken ties and other stories, 1925
- Rabindranath tagore: Twenty-two poems, 1925
- Rakta-karabi, 1925 - red oleanders
- Sadhana, 1926 - suom.
- Natir puja, 1926 - transl.
- Letters to a friend, 1928
- Sesher kavita, 1929 - farewell, my friend
- Mahua, 1929 - the herald of spring
- Jatri, 1929
- Yagayog, 1929
- The religion of man, 1930
- The child, 1931
- Rashiar chithi, 1931 - letters from russia
- Patraput, 1932
- Punascha, 1932
- Mahatmahi and the depressed humanity, 1932
- The golden boat, 1932
- Sheaves, poems and songs, 1932

- Dui bon, 1933 - two sisters
- Chandalika, 1933 - transl.
- Malancha, 1934 - the garden
- Char adhyaya, 1934 - four chapters
- Bithika, 1935
- Shesh saptak, 1935
- Patraput, 1936
- Syamali, 1936 - trans.
- Collected poems and plays, 1936
- Khapchara, 1937
- Semjuti, 1938
- Prantik, 1938
- Prahasini, 1939
- Pather sancay, 1939
- Akaspradip, 1939
- Syama, 1939
- Nabajatak, 1940
- Shanai, 1940
- Chelebela, 1940 - my boyhood days
- Rogshajyay, 1940
- Arogya, 1941
- Janmadine, 1941
- Galpasalpa, 1941
- Last poems, 1941
- The parrots training, 1944
- Rolland and tagore, 1945
- Three plays, 1950
- Crisis in civilization, 1950
- Sheaves, 1951
- More stories from tagore, 1951
- A tagore's testament, 1955
- Our universe, 1958
- The runaway and other stories, 1959
- Wings of death, 1960
- Gitabitan, 1960
- A tagore reader, 1961 (ed. By amiya chakravarty)
- Towards universal man, 1961
- On art and aesthetics, 1961

- Bicitra, 1961
- Galpaguccha, 1960-62 (4 vols.)
- Boundless sky, 1964
- The housewarming, 1964
- Rabindra-racanabali, 1964-1966 (27 vols.)
- Patraput, 1969
- Imperfect encounter, 1972
- Later poems, 1974
- The housewarming, 1977
- Rabindranath tagore: Selected poems, 1985
- Rabindranath tagore: Selected short stories, 1991 (trans. By william radice)

Chapter 4

Presentation Speech

Presentation Speech by Harald Hjärne, Chairman of the Nobel Committee of the Swedish Academy, on December 10, 1913.

In awarding the Nobel Prize in Literature to the Anglo-Indian poet, Rabindranath Tagore, the Academy has found itself in the happy position of being able to accord this recognition to an author who, in conformity with the express wording of Alfred Nobel's last will and testament, had during the current year, written the finest poems «of an idealistic tendency.» Moreover, after exhaustive and conscientious deliberation, having concluded that these poems of his most nearly approach the prescribed standard, the Academy thought that there was no reason to hesitate because the poet's name was still comparatively unknown in Europe, due to the distant location of his home. There was even less reason since the founder of the Prize laid it down in set terms as his «express wish and desire that, in the awarding of the Prize, no consideration should be paid to the nationality to which any proposed candidate might belong.»

Tagore's *Gitanjali: Song Offerings* (1912), a collection of religious poems, was the one of his works that especially arrested the attention of the selecting critics. Since last year the book, in a real and full sense, has belonged to English literature, for the author himself, who by education and practice is a poet in his native Indian tongue, has bestowed upon the poems a new dress, alike perfect in form and personally original in inspiration. This has made them accessible to all in England, America, and the entire Western world for whom noble literature is of interest and moment. Quite independently of any knowledge of his Bengali poetry, irrespective, too, of differences of religious faiths, literary schools, or party aims, Tagore has been hailed from various quarters as a new and admirable master of that poetic art which has been a never-failing concomitant of the expansion of British civilization ever since the days of Queen Elizabeth. The features of this poetry that won immediate and enthusiastic admiration are the perfection with which the poet's own ideas and those he has borrowed have been harmonized into a complete whole; his rhythmically balanced style, that, to quote an English critic's opinion, «combines at once the feminine grace of poetry with the virile power of prose»; his austere, by some termed classic, taste in the choice of words and his use of the other elements of expression in a borrowed tongue - those features, in short, that stamp an original work as such, but which at the same time render more difficult its reproduction in another language.

The same estimate is true of the second cycle of poems that came before us, *The Gardener, Lyrics of Love and Life* (1913). In this work, however, as the author himself points out, he has recast rather than interpreted his earlier inspirations. Here we see another phase of his personality, now subject to the alternately blissful and torturing experiences of youthful love, now prey to the feelings of longing and joy that the vicissitudes of life give rise to, the whole interspersed nevertheless with glimpses of a higher world.

English translations of Tagore's prose stories have been published under the title *Glimpses of Bengal Life* (1913). Though the form of these tales does not bear his own stamp - the rendering being by another hand - their content gives evidence of his versatility and wide range of observation, of his heartfelt sympathy with the fates and experiences of differing types of men, and of his talent for plot construction and development.

Tagore has since published both a collection of poems, poetic pictures of childhood and home life, symbolically entitled *The Crescent Moon* (1913), and a number of lectures given before American and English university audiences, which in book form he calls *Sâdhanâ: The Realisation of Life* (1913). They embody his views of the ways in which man can arrive at a faith in the light of which it may be possible to live. This very seeking of his to discover the true relation between faith and thought makes Tagore stand out as a poet of rich endowment, characterized by his great profundity of thought, but most of all by his warmth of feeling and by the moving power of his figurative language. Seldom indeed in the realm of imaginative literature are attained so great a range and diversity of note and of colour, capable of expressing with equal harmony and grace the emotions of every mood from the longing of the soul after eternity to the joyous merriment prompted by the innocent child at play.

Concerning our understanding of this poetry, by no means exotic but truly universally human in character, the future will probably add to what we know now. We do know, however, that the poet's motivation extends to the effort of reconciling two spheres of civilization widely separated, which above all is the characteristic mark of our present epoch and constitutes its most important task and problem. The true inwardness of this work is most clearly and purely revealed in the efforts exerted in the Christian mission-field throughout the world. In times to come, historical inquirers will know better how to appraise its importance and influence, even in what is at present hidden from our gaze and where no or only grudging recognition is accorded.

They will undoubtedly form a higher estimate of it than the one now deemed fitting in many quarters. Thanks to this movement, fresh, bubbling springs of living water have been tapped, from which poetry in particular may draw inspiration, even though those springs are perhaps intermingled with alien streams, and whether or not they be traced to their right source or their origin be attributed to the depths of the dreamworld. More especially, the preaching of the Christian religion has provided in many places the first definite impulse toward a revival and regeneration of the vernacular language, i.e., its liberation from the bondage of an artificial tradition, and consequently also toward a development of its capacity for nurturing and sustaining a vein of living and natural poetry. The Christian mission has exercised its influence as a rejuvenating force in India, too, where in conjunction with religious revivals many of the vernaculars were early put to literary use, thereby acquiring status and stability. However, with only too regular frequency, they fossilized again under pressure from the new tradition that gradually established itself. But the influence of the Christian mission has extended far beyond the range of the actually registered proselytizing work. The struggle that the last century witnessed between the living vernaculars and the sacred language of ancient times for control over the new literatures springing into life would have had a very different course and outcome, had not the former found able support in the fostering care bestowed upon them by the self-sacrificing missionaries.

It was in Bengal, the oldest Anglo-Indian province and the scene many years before of the indefatigable labours of that missionary pioneer, Carey, to promote the Christian religion and to improve the vernacular language, that Rabindranath Tagore was born in 1861. He was a scion of a respected family that had already given evidence of intellectual ability in many areas. The surroundings in which the boy and young man grew up were in no sense primitive or calculated to hem in his conceptions of the world and of life. On the contrary, in his home there prevailed, along with a highly cultivated appreciation of art, a profound reverence for the inquiring spirit and wisdom of the forefathers of the race, whose texts were used for family devotional worship. Around him, too, there was then coming into being a new literary spirit that consciously sought to reach forth to the people and to make itself acquainted with their life needs. This new spirit gained in force as reforms ere firmly effected by the Government, after the quelling of the widespread, confused Indian Mutiny.

Rabindranath's father was one of the leading and most zealous members of a religious community to which his son still belongs. That body, known by the name of «Brahmo Samaj», did not arise as a sect of the ancient Hindu type, with the purpose of spreading the worship of some particular godhead as superior to all others. Rather, it was founded in the early part of the nineteenth century by an enlightened and influential man who had been much impressed by the doctrines of Christianity, which he had studied also in England. He endeavoured to give to the native Hindu traditions, handed down from the past, an interpretation in agreement with what he conceived to be the spirit and import of the Christian faith.

Doctrinal controversy has since been rife regarding the interpretation of truth that he and his successors were thus led to give, whereby the community has been subdivided into a number of independent sects. The character, too, of the community, appealing essentially to highly trained intellectual minds, has from its inception always precluded any large growth of the numbers of its avowed adherents. Nevertheless, the indirect influence exercised by the body, even upon the development of popular education and literature, is held to be very considerable indeed. Among those community members who have grown up in recent years, Rabindranath Tagore has laboured to a pre-eminent degree. To them he has stood as a revered master and prophet. That intimate interplay of teacher and pupil so earnestly sought after has attained a deep, hearty, and simple manifestation, both in religious life and in literary training.

To carry out his life's work Tagore equipped himself with a many-sided culture, European as well as Indian, extended and matured by travels abroad and by advanced study in London. In his youth he travelled widely in his own land, accompanying his father as far as the Himalayas. He was still quite young when he began to write in Bengali, and he has tried his hand in prose and poetry, lyrics and dramas. In addition to his descriptions of the life of he common people of his own country, he has dealt in separate works with questions in literary criticism, philosophy, and sociology. At one period, some time ago, there occurred a break in the busy round of his activities, for he then felt obliged, in accord with immemorial practice among his race, to pursue for a time a contemplative hermit life in a boat floating on the waters of a tributary of the sacred Ganges River. After he returned to ordinary life, his reputation among his own people as a man of refined wisdom and chastened piety grew greater from day to day. The open-air school which he established in western Bengal, beneath the sheltering branches of the mango tree, has brought up numbers of youths who as devoted disciples have spread his teaching throughout the land. To this place he has now retired, after spending nearly a year as an honoured guest in the literary circles of England and America and attending the Religious History Congress held in Paris last summer .

Wherever Tagore has encountered minds open to receive his high teaching, the reception accorded him has been that suited to a bearer of good tidings which are delivered, in language intelligible to all, from that treasure house of the East whose existence had long been conjectured. His own attitude, moreover, is that he is but the intermediary, giving freely of that to which by birth he has access. He is not at all anxious to shine before men as a genius or as an inventor of some new thing. In contrast to the cult of work, which is the product of life in the fenced-in cities of the Western world, with its fostering of a restless, contentious spirit; in contrast to its struggle to conquer nature for the love of gain and profit, «as if we are living», Tagore says, «in a hostile world where we have to wrest everything we want from an unwilling and alien arrangement of things» (*Sâdhanâ*, p. 5); in contrast to all that enervating hurry and scurry, he places before us the culture that in the vast, peaceful, and enshrining forests of India attains its perfection, a culture that seeks primarily the quiet peace of the soul in ever-increasing harmony with the life of nature herself It is a poetical, not a historical, picture that Tagore here reveals to us to confirm his promise that a peace awaits us, too. By virtue of the right associated with the gift of prophecy, he freely depicts the scenes that have loomed before his creative vision at a period contemporary with the beginning of time.

He is, however, as far removed as anyone in our midst from all that we are accustomed to hear dispensed and purveyed in the market places as Oriental philosophy, from painful dreams about the transmigration of souls and the impersonal *karma,* from the pantheistic, and in reality abstract, belief that is usually regarded as peculiarly characteristic of the higher civilization in India. Tagore himself is not even prepared to admit that a belief of that description can claim any authority from the profoundest utterances of the wise men of the past. He peruses his Vedic hymns, his *Upanishads,* and indeed the theses of Buddha himself, in such a manner that he discovers in them, what is for him an irrefutable truth.

If he seeks the divinity in nature, he finds there a living personality with the features of omnipotence, the all-embracing lord of nature, whose preternatural spiritual power nevertheless likewise reveals its presence in all temporal life, small as well as great, but especially in the soul of man predestined for eternity. Praise, prayer, and fervent devotion pervade the song offerings that he lays at the feet of this nameless divinity of his. Ascetic and even ethic austerity would appear to be alien to his type of divinity worship, which may be characterized as a species of aesthetic theism. Piety of that description is in full concord with the whole of his poetry, and it has bestowed peace upon him. He proclaims the coming of that peace for weary and careworn souls even within the bounds of Christendom.

This is mysticism, if we like to call it so, but not a mysticism that, relinquishing personality, seeks to become absorbed in an All that approaches a Nothingness, but one that, with all the talents and faculties of the soul trained to their highest pitch, eagerly sets forth to meet the living Father of the whole creation. This more strenuous type of mysticism was not wholly unknown even in India before the days of Tagore, hardly indeed among the ascetics and philosophers of ancient times but rather in the many forms of *bhakti,* a piety whose very essence is the profound love of and reliance upon God. Ever since the Middle Ages, influenced in some measure by the Christian and other foreign religions, *bhakti* has sought the ideals of its faith in the different phases of Hinduism, varied in character but each to all intents monotheistic in conception.

All those higher forms of faith have disappeared or have been depraved past recognition, choked by the superabundant growth of that mixture of cults that has attracted to its banner all those Indian peoples who lacked an adequate power of resistance to its blandishments. Even though Tagore may have borrowed one or another note from the orchestral symphonies of his native predecessors, yet he treads upon firmer ground in this age that draws the peoples of the earth closer together along paths of peace, and of strife too, to joint and collective responsibilities, and that spends its own energies in dispatching greetings and good wishes far over land and sea. Tagore, though, in thought-impelling pictures, has shown us how all things temporal are swallowed up in the eternal:

Time is endless in thy hands, my lord.

There is none to count thy minutes.

Days and nights pass and ages bloom and fade like flowers. Thou knowest how to wait.

Thy centuries follow each other perfecting a small wild flower. We have no time to lose, and having no time, we must scramble for our chances. We are too poor to be late.

And thus it is that time goes try, while I give it to every querulous man who claims it, and thine altar is empty of all offerings to the last. At the end of the day I hasten in fear lest thy gate be shut; but if I find that yet there is time.

Chapter 5

Complete Text

RABINDRANATH TAGORE
GITANJALI
Song Offerings
A collection of prose translations
made by the author from
the original Bengali
With an introduction by
W. B. YEATS
to WILLIAM ROTHENSTEIN
INTRODUCTION

A few days ago I said to a distinguished Bengali doctor of medicine, 'I know no German, yet if a translation of a German poet had moved me, I would go to the British Museum and find books in English that would tell me something of his life, and of the history of his thought. But though these prose translations from Rabindranath Tagore have stirred my blood as nothing has for years, I shall not know anything of his life, and of the movements of thought that have made them possible, if some Indian traveller will not tell me.' It seemed to him natural that I should be moved, for he said, 'I read Rabindranath every day, to read one line of his is to forget all the troubles of the world.' I said, 'An Englishman living in London in the reign of Richard the Second had he been shown translations from Petrarch or from Dante, would have found no books to answer his questions, but would have questioned some Florentine banker or Lombard merchant as I question you. For all I know, so abundant and simple is this poetry, the new renaissance has been born in your country and I shall never know of it except by hearsay.' He answered, 'We have other poets, but none that are his equal; we call this the epoch of Rabindranath. No poet seems to me as famous in Europe as he is among us. He is as great in music as in poetry, and his songs are sung from the west of India into Burma wherever Bengali is spoken. He was already famous at nineteen when he wrote his first novel; and plays when he was but little older, are still played in Calcutta.

I so much admire the completeness of his life; when he was very young he wrote much of natural objects, he would sit all day in his garden; from his twenty-fifth year or so to his thirty-fifth perhaps, when he had a great sorrow, he wrote the most beautiful love poetry in our language'; and then he said with deep emotion, 'words can never express what I owed at seventeen to his love poetry. After that his art grew deeper, it became religious and philosophical; all the inspiration of mankind are in his hymns. He is the first among our saints who has not refused to live, but has spoken out of Life itself, and that is why we give him our love.' I may have changed his well-chosen words in my memory but not his thought. 'A little while ago he was to read divine service in one of our churches—we of the Brahma Samaj use your word 'church' in English—it was the largest in Calcutta and not only was it crowded, but the streets were all but impassable because of the people.'

Other Indians came to see me and their reverence for this man sounded strange in our world, where we hide great and little things under the same veil of obvious comedy and half-serious depreciation. When we were making the cathedrals had we a like reverence for our great men? 'Every morning at three—I know, for I have seen it'—one said to me, 'he sits immovable in contemplation, and for two hours does not awake from his reverie upon the nature of God. His father, the Maha Rishi, would sometimes sit there all through the next day; once, upon a river, he fell into contemplation because of the beauty of the landscape, and the rowers waited for eight hours before they could continue their journey.' He then told me of Mr. Tagore's family and how for generations great men have come out of its cradles. 'Today,' he said, 'there are Gogonendranath and Abanindranath Tagore, who are artists; and Dwijendranath, Rabindranath's brother, who is a great philosopher. The squirrels come from the boughs and climb on to his knees and the birds alight upon his hands.' I notice in these men's thought a sense of visible beauty and meaning as though they held that doctrine of Nietzsche that we must not believe in the moral or intellectual beauty which does not sooner or later impress itself upon physical things.

I said, 'In the East you know how to keep a family illustrious. The other day the curator of a museum pointed out to me a little dark-skinned man who was arranging their Chinese prints and said, "That is the hereditary connoisseur of the Mikado, he is the fourteenth of his family to hold the post." 'He answered, 'When Rabindranath was a boy he had all round him in his home literature and music.' I thought of the abundance, of the simplicity of the poems, and said, 'In your country is there much propagandist writing, much criticism? We have to do so much, especially in my own country, that our minds gradually cease to be creative, and yet we cannot help it.

If our life was not a continual warfare, we would not have taste, we would not know what is good, we would not find hearers and readers. Four-fifths of our energy is spent in the quarrel with bad taste, whether in our own minds or in the minds of others.' 'I understand,' he replied, 'we too have our propagandist writing. In the villages they recite long mythological poems adapted from the Sanskrit in the Middle Ages, and they often insert passages telling the people that they must do their duties.'

I have carried the manuscript of these translations about with me for days, reading it in railway trains, or on the top of omnibuses and in restaurants, and I have often had to close it lest some stranger would see how much it moved me. These lyrics—which are in the original, my Indians tell me, full of subtlety of rhythm, of untranslatable delicacies of colour, of metrical invention—display in their thought a world I have dreamed of all my live long. The work of a supreme culture, they yet appear as much the growth of the common soil as the grass and the rushes. A tradition, where poetry and religion are the same thing, has passed through the centuries, gathering from learned and unlearned metaphor and emotion, and carried back again to the multitude the thought of the scholar and of the noble. If the civilization of Bengal remains unbroken, if that common mind which—as one divines—runs through all, is not, as with us, broken into a dozen minds that know nothing of each other, something even of what is most subtle in these verses will have come, in a few generations, to the beggar on the roads. When there was but one mind in England, Chaucer wrote his *Troilus and Cressida,* and thought he had written to be read, or to be read out—for our time was coming on apace—he was sung by minstrels for a while.

Rabindranath Tagore, like Chaucer's forerunners, writes music for his words, and one understands at every moment that he is so abundant, so spontaneous, so daring in his passion, so full of surprise, because he is doing something which has never seemed strange, unnatural, or in need of defence. These verses will not lie in little well-printed books upon ladies' tables, who turn the pages with indolent hands that they may sigh over a life without meaning, which is yet all they can know of life, or be carried by students at the university to be laid aside when the work of life begins, but, as the generations pass, travellers will hum them on the highway and men rowing upon the rivers. Lovers, while they await one another, shall find, in murmuring them, this love of God a magic gulf wherein their own more bitter passion may bathe and renew its youth.

At every moment the heart of this poet flows outward to these without derogation or condescension, for it has known that they will understand; and it has filled itself with the circumstance of their lives. The traveller in the read-brown clothes that he wears that dust may not show upon him, the girl searching in her bed for the petals fallen from the wreath of her royal lover, the servant or the bride awaiting the master's home-coming in the empty house, are images of the heart turning to God. Flowers and rivers, the blowing of conch shells, the heavy rain of the Indian July, or the moods of that heart in union or in separation; and a man sitting in a boat upon a river playing lute, like one of those figures full of mysterious meaning in a Chinese picture, is God Himself. A whole people, a whole civilization, immeasurably strange to us, seems to have been taken up into this imagination; and yet we are not moved because of its strangeness, but because we have met our own image, as though we had walked in Rossetti's willow wood, or heard, perhaps for the first time in literature, our voice as in a dream.

Since the Renaissance the writing of European saints—however familiar their metaphor and the general structure of their thought—has ceased to hold our attention. We know that we must at last forsake the world, and we are accustomed in moments of weariness or exaltation to consider a voluntary forsaking; but how can we, who have read so much poetry, seen so many paintings, listened to so much music, where the cry of the flesh and the cry of the soul seems one, forsake it harshly and rudely? What have we in common with St. Bernard covering his eyes that they may not dwell upon the beauty of the lakes of Switzerland, or with the violent rhetoric of the Book of Revelations? We would, if we might, find, as in this book, words full of courtesy. 'I have got my leave. Bid me farewell, my brothers! I bow to you all and take my departure. Here I give back the keys of my door—and I give up all claims to my house. I only ask for last kind words from you.

We were neighbours for long, but I received more than I could give. Now the day has dawned and the lamp that lit my dark corner is out. A summons has come and I am ready for my journey.' And it is our own mood, when it is furthest from 'a Kempis or John of the Cross, that cries, 'And because I love this life, I know I shall love death as well.' Yet it is not only in our thoughts of the parting that this book fathoms all. We had not known that we loved God, hardly it may be that we believed in Him; yet looking backward upon our life we discover, in our exploration of the pathways of woods, in our delight in the lonely places of hills, in that mysterious claim that we have made, unavailingly on the woman that we have loved, the emotion that created this insidious sweetness. 'Entering my heart unbidden even as one of the common crowd, unknown to me, my king, thou didst press the signet of eternity upon many a fleeting moment.' This is no longer the sanctity of the cell and of the scourge; being but a lifting up, as it were, into a greater intensity of the mood of the painter, painting the dust and the sunlight, and we go for a like voice to St. Francis and to William Blake who have seemed so alien in our violent history.

We write long books where no page perhaps has any quality to make writing a pleasure, being confident in some general design, just as we fight and make money and fill our heads with politics—all dull things in the doing—while Mr. Tagore, like the Indian civilization itself, has been content to discover the soul and surrender himself to its spontaneity. He often seems to contrast life with that of those who have loved more after our fashion, and have more seeming weight in the world, and always humbly as though he were only sure his way is best for him: 'Men going home glance at me and smile and fill me with shame. I sit like a beggar maid, drawing my skirt over my face, and when they ask me, what it is I want, I drop my eyes and answer them not.' At another time, remembering how his life had once a different shape, he will say, 'Many an hour I have spent in the strife of the good and the evil, but now it is the pleasure of my playmate of the empty days to draw my heart on to him; and I know not why this sudden call to what useless inconsequence.'

An innocence, a simplicity that one does not find elsewhere in literature makes the birds and the leaves seem as near to him as they are near to children, and the changes of the seasons great events as before our thoughts had arisen between them and us. At times I wonder if he has it from the literature of Bengal or from religion, and at other times, remembering the birds alighting on his brother's hands, I find pleasure in thinking it hereditary, a mystery that was growing through the centuries like the courtesy of a Tristan or a Pelanore. Indeed, when he is speaking of children, so much a part of himself this quality seems, one is not certain that he is not also speaking of the saints, 'They build their houses with sand and they play with empty shells. With withered leaves they weave their boats and smilingly float them on the vast deep. Children have their play on the seashore of worlds. They know not how to swim, they know not how to cast nets. Pearl fishers dive for pearls, merchants sail in their ships, while children gather pebbles and scatter them again. They seek not for hidden treasures, they know not how to cast nets.'

W.B. YEATS *September 1912*

GITANJALI

Thou hast made me endless, such is thy pleasure. This frail vessel thou emptiest again and again, and fillest it ever with fresh life.

This little flute of a reed thou hast carried over hills and dales, and hast breathed through it melodies eternally new.

At the immortal touch of thy hands my little heart loses its limits in joy and gives birth to utterance ineffable.

Thy infinite gifts come to me only on these very small hands of mine. Ages pass, and still thou pourest, and still there is room to fill.

When thou commandest me to sing it seems that my heart would break with pride; and I look to thy face, and tears come to my eyes.

All that is harsh and dissonant in my life melts into one sweet harmony—and my adoration spreads wings like a glad bird on its flight across the sea.

I know thou takest pleasure in my singing. I know that only as a singer I come before thy presence.

I touch by the edge of the far-spreading wing of my song thy feet which I could never aspire to reach.

Drunk with the joy of singing I forget myself and call thee friend who art my lord.

I know not how thou singest, my master! I ever listen in silent amazement.

The light of thy music illumines the world. The life breath of thy music runs from sky to sky. The holy stream of thy music breaks through all stony obstacles and rushes on.

My heart longs to join in thy song, but vainly struggles for a voice. I would speak, but speech breaks not into song, and I cry out baffled. Ah, thou hast made my heart captive in the endless meshes of thy music, my master!

Life of my life, I shall ever try to keep my body pure, knowing that thy living touch is upon all my limbs.

I shall ever try to keep all untruths out from my thoughts, knowing that thou art that truth which has kindled the light of reason in my mind.

I shall ever try to drive all evils away from my heart and keep my love in flower, knowing that thou hast thy seat in the inmost shrine of my heart.

And it shall be my endeavour to reveal thee in my actions, knowing it is thy power gives me strength to act.

I ask for a moment's indulgence to sit by thy side. The works that I have in hand I will finish afterwards.

Away from the sight of thy face my heart knows no rest nor respite, and my work becomes an endless toil in a shoreless sea of toil.

Today the summer has come at my window with its sighs and murmurs; and the bees are plying their minstrelsy at the court of the flowering grove.

Now it is time to sit quite, face to face with thee, and to sing dedication of live in this silent and overflowing leisure.

Pluck this little flower and take it, delay not! I fear lest it droop and drop into the dust.

I may not find a place in thy garland, but honour it with a touch of pain from thy hand and pluck it. I fear lest the day end before I am aware, and the time of offering go by.

Though its colour be not deep and its smell be faint, use this flower in thy service and pluck it while there is time.

My song has put off her adornments. She has no pride of dress and decoration. Ornaments would mar our union; they would come between thee and me; their jingling would drown thy whispers.

My poet's vanity dies in shame before thy sight. O master poet, I have sat down at thy feet. Only let me make my life simple and straight, like a flute of reed for thee to fill with music. The child who is decked with prince's robes and who has jewelled chains round his neck loses all pleasure in his play; his dress hampers him at every step.

In fear that it may be frayed, or stained with dust he keeps himself from the world, and is afraid even to move.

Mother, it is no gain, thy bondage of finery, if it keep one shut off from the healthful dust of the earth, if it rob one of the right of entrance to the great fair of common human life.

O Fool, try to carry thyself upon thy own shoulders! O beggar, to come beg at thy own door!

Leave all thy burdens on his hands who can bear all, and never look behind in regret.

Thy desire at once puts out the light from the lamp it touches with its breath. It is unholy—take not thy gifts through its unclean hands. Accept only what is offered by sacred love.

Here is thy footstool and there rest thy feet where live the poorest, and lowliest, and lost.

When I try to bow to thee, my obeisance cannot reach down to the depth where thy feet rest among the poorest, and lowliest, and lost.

Pride can never approach to where thou walkest in the clothes of the humble among the poorest, and lowliest, and lost.

My heart can never find its way to where thou keepest company with the companionless among the poorest, the lowliest, and the lost.

Leave this chanting and singing and telling of beads! Whom dost thou worship in this lonely dark corner of a temple with doors all shut? Open thine eyes and see thy God is not before thee!

He is there where the tiller is tilling the hard ground and where the pathmaker is breaking stones. He is with them in sun and in shower, and his garment is covered with dust. Put of thy holy mantle and even like him come down on the dusty soil!

Deliverance? Where is this deliverance to be found? Our master himself has joyfully taken upon him the bonds of creation; he is bound with us all for ever.

Come out of thy meditations and leave aside thy flowers and incense! What harm is there if thy clothes become tattered and stained? Meet him and stand by him in toil and in sweat of thy brow.

The time that my journey takes is long and the way of it long.

I came out on the chariot of the first gleam of light, and pursued my voyage through the wildernesses of worlds leaving my track on many a star and planet.

It is the most distant course that comes nearest to thyself, and that training is the most intricate which leads to the utter simplicity of a tune.

The traveller has to knock at every alien door to come to his own, and one has to wander through all the outer worlds to reach the innermost shrine at the end.

My eyes strayed far and wide before I shut them and said 'Here art thou!'

The question and the cry 'Oh, where?' melt into tears of a thousand streams and deluge the world with the flood of the assurance 'I am!'

The song that I came to sing remains unsung to this day.

I have spent my days in stringing and in unstringing my instrument.

The time has not come true, the words have not been rightly set; only there is the agony of wishing in my heart.

The blossom has not opened; only the wind is sighing by.

I have not seen his face, nor have I listened to his voice; only I have heard his gentle footsteps from the road before my house.

The livelong day has passed in spreading his seat on the floor; but the lamp has not been lit and I cannot ask him into my house.

I live in the hope of meeting with him; but this meeting is not yet.

My desires are many and my cry is pitiful, but ever didst thou save me by hard refusals; and this strong mercy has been wrought into my life through and through.

Day by day thou art making me worthy of the simple,

great gifts that thou gavest to me unasked—this sky and the light, this body and the life and the mind—saving me from perils of overmuch desire.

There are times when I languidly linger and times when I awaken and hurry in search of my goal; but cruelly thou hidest thyself from before me.

Day by day thou art making me worthy of thy full acceptance by refusing me ever and anon, saving me from perils of weak, uncertain desire.

I am here to sing thee songs. In this hall of thine I have a corner seat.

In thy world I have no work to do; my useless life can only break out in tunes without a purpose.

When the hour strikes for thy silent worship at the dark temple of midnight, command me, my master, to stand before thee to sing.

When in the morning air the golden harp is tuned, honour me, commanding my presence.

I have had my invitation to this world's festival, and thus my life has been blessed. My eyes have seen and my ears have heard.

It was my part at this feast to play upon my instrument, and I have done all I could.

Now, I ask, has the time come at last when I may go in and see thy face and offer thee my silent salutation?

I am only waiting for love to give myself up at last into his hands. That is why it is so late and why I have been guilty of such omissions.

They come with their laws and their codes to bind me fast; but I evade them ever, for I am only waiting for love to give myself up at last into his hands.

People blame me and call me heedless; I doubt not they are right in their blame.

The market day is over and work is all done for the busy. Those who came to call me in vain have gone back in anger. I am only waiting for love to give myself up at last into his hands. Clouds heap upon clouds and it darkens. Ah, love, why dost thou let me wait outside at the door all alone?

In the busy moments of the noontide work I am with the crowd, but on this dark lonely day it is only for thee that I hope. If thou showest me not thy face, if thou leavest me wholly aside, I know not how I am to pass these long, rainy hours.

I keep gazing on the far-away gloom of the sky, and my heart wanders wailing with the restless wind.

If thou speakest not I will fill my heart with thy silence and endure it. I will keep still and wait like the night with starry vigil and its head bent low with patience.

The morning will surely come, the darkness will vanish, and thy voice pour down in golden streams breaking through the sky.

Then thy words will take wing in songs from every one of my birds' nests, and thy melodies will break forth in flowers in all my forest groves.

On the day when the lotus bloomed, alas, my mind was straying, and I knew it not. My basket was empty and the flower remained unheeded.

Only now and again a sadness fell upon me, and I started up from my dream and felt a sweet trace of a strange fragrance in the south wind.

That vague sweetness made my heart ache with longing and it seemed to me that is was the eager breath of the summer seeking for its completion.

I knew not then that it was so near, that it was mine, and that this perfect sweetness had blossomed in the depth of my own heart.

I must launch out my boat. The languid hours pass by on the shore—Alas for me!

The spring has done its flowering and taken leave. And now with the burden of faded futile flowers I wait and linger.

The waves have become clamorous, and upon the bank in the shady lane the yellow leaves flutter and fall.

What emptiness do you gaze upon! Do you not feel a thrill passing through the air with the notes of the far-away song floating from the other shore?

In the deep shadows of the rainy July, with secret steps,

thou walkest, silent as night, eluding all watchers. Today the morning has closed its eyes, heedless of the insistent calls of the loud east wind, and a thick veil has been drawn over the ever-wakeful blue sky.

The woodlands have hushed their songs, and doors are all shut at every house. Thou art the solitary wayfarer in this deserted street. Oh my only friend, my best beloved, the gates are open in my house—do not pass by like a dream.

Art thou abroad on this stormy night on thy journey of love, my friend? The sky groans like one in despair.

I have no sleep tonight. Ever and again I open my door and look out on the darkness, my friend!

I can see nothing before me. I wonder where lies thy path!

By what dim shore of the ink-black river, by what far edge of the frowning forest, through what mazy depth of gloom art thou threading thy course to come to me, my friend?

If the day is done, if birds sing no more, if the wind has flagged tired, then draw the veil of darkness thick upon me, even as thou hast wrapt the earth with the coverlet of sleep and tenderly closed the petals of the drooping lotus at dusk.

From the traveller, whose sack of provisions is empty before the voyage is ended, whose garment is torn and dustladen, whose strength is exhausted, remove shame and poverty, and renew his life like a flower under the cover of thy kindly night.

In the night of weariness let me give myself up to sleep without struggle, resting my trust upon thee.

Let me not force my flagging spirit into a poor preparation for thy worship.

It is thou who drawest the veil of night upon the tired eyes of the day to renew its sight in a fresher gladness of awakening.

He came and sat by my side but I woke not. What a cursed sleep it was, O miserable me!

He came when the night was still; he had his harp in his hands, and my dreams became resonant with its melodies.

Alas, why are my nights all thus lost? Ah, why do I ever miss his sight whose breath touches my sleep?

Light, oh where is the light? Kindle it with the burning fire of desire! There is the lamp but never a flicker of a flame—is such thy fate, my heart? Ah, death were better by far for thee! Misery knocks at thy door, and her message is that thy lord is wakeful, and he calls thee to the love-tryst through the darkness of night.

The sky is overcast with clouds and the rain is ceaseless. I know not what this is that stirs in me—I know not its meaning.

A moment's flash of lightning drags down a deeper gloom on my sight, and my heart gropes for the path to where the music of the night calls me.

Light, oh where is the light! Kindle it with the burning fire of desire! It thunders and the wind rushes screaming through the void. The night is black as a black stone. Let not the hours pass by in the dark. Kindle the lamp of love with thy life.

Obstinate are the trammels, but my heart aches when I try to break them.

Freedom is all I want, but to hope for it I feel ashamed.

I am certain that priceless wealth is in thee, and that thou art my best friend, but I have not the heart to sweep away the tinsel that fills my room

The shroud that covers me is a shroud of dust and death; I hate it, yet hug it in love.

My debts are large, my failures great, my shame secret and heavy; yet when I come to ask for my good, I quake in fear lest my prayer be granted.

He whom I enclose with my name is weeping in this dungeon. I am ever busy building this wall all around; and as this wall goes up into the sky day by day I lose sight of my true being in its dark shadow.

I take pride in this great wall, and I plaster it with dust and sand lest a least hole should be left in this name; and for all the care I take I lose sight of my true being.

I came out alone on my way to my tryst. But who is this that follows me in the silent dark?

I move aside to avoid his presence but I escape him not.

He makes the dust rise from the earth with his swagger; he adds his loud voice to every word that I utter.

He is my own little self, my lord, he knows no shame; but I am ashamed to come to thy door in his company.

'Prisoner, tell me, who was it that bound you?'

'It was my master,' said the prisoner. 'I thought I could outdo everybody in the world in wealth and power, and I amassed in my own treasure-house the money due to my king. When sleep overcame me I lay upon the bed that was for my lord, and on waking up I found I was a prisoner in my own treasure-house.'

'Prisoner, tell me, who was it that wrought this unbreakable chain?'

'It was I,' said the prisoner, 'who forged this chain very carefully. I thought my invincible power would hold the world captive leaving me in a freedom undisturbed. Thus night and day I worked at the chain with huge fires and cruel hard strokes. When at last the work was done and the links were complete and unbreakable, I found that it held me in its grip.'

By all means they try to hold me secure who love me in this world. But it is otherwise with thy love which is greater than theirs, and thou keepest me free.

Lest I forget them they never venture to leave me alone. But day passes by after day and thou art not seen.

If I call not thee in my prayers, if I keep not thee in my heart, thy love for me still waits for my love.

When it was day they came into my house and said, 'We shall only take the smallest room here.'

They said, 'We shall help you in the worship of your God and humbly accept only our own share in his grace'; and then they took their seat in a corner and they sat quiet and meek.

But in the darkness of night I find they break into my sacred shrine, strong and turbulent, and snatch with unholy greed the offerings from God's altar. Let only that little be left of me whereby I may name thee my all.

Let only that little be left of my will whereby I may feel thee on every side, and come to thee in everything, and offer to thee my love every moment.

Let only that little be left of me whereby I may never hide thee. Let only that little of my fetters be left whereby I am bound with thy will, and thy purpose is carried out in my life—and that is the fetter of thy love.

Where the mind is without fear and the head is held high;

Where knowledge is free;

Where the world has not been broken up into fragments by narrow domestic walls;

Where words come out from the depth of truth;

Where tireless striving stretches its arms towards perfection;

Where the clear stream of reason has not lost its way into the dreary desert sand of dead habit;

Where the mind is led forward by thee into ever-widening thought and action—

Into that heaven of freedom, my Father, let my country awake.

This is my prayer to thee, my lord—strike, strike at the root of penury in my heart.

Give me the strength lightly to bear my joys and sorrows.

Give me the strength to make my love fruitful in service.

Give me the strength never to disown the poor or bend my knees before insolent might.

Give me the strength to raise my mind high above daily trifles. And give me the strength to surrender my strength to thy will with love.

I thought that my voyage had come to its end at the last limit of my power,—that the path before me was closed, that provisions were exhausted and the time come to take shelter in a silent obscurity.

But I find that thy will knows no end in me. And when old words die out on the tongue, new melodies break forth from the heart; and where the old tracks are lost, new country is revealed with its wonders.

That I want thee, only thee—let my heart repeat without end. All desires that distract me, day and night, are false and empty to the core.

As the night keeps hidden in its gloom the petition for

light, even thus in the depth of my unconsciousness rings the cry—'I want thee, only thee'.

As the storm still seeks its end in peace when it strikes against peace with all its might, even thus my rebellion strikes against thy love and still its cry is—'I want thee, only thee'.

When the heart is hard and parched up, come upon me with a shower of mercy.

When grace is lost from life, come with a burst of song.

When tumultuous work raises its din on all sides shutting me out from beyond, come to me, my lord of silence, with thy peace and rest. When my beggarly heart sits crouched, shut up in a corner, break open the door, my king, and come with the ceremony of a king.

When desire blinds the mind with delusion and dust, O thou holy one, thou wakeful, come with thy light and thy thunder.

The rain has held back for days and days, my God, in my arid heart. The horizon is fiercely naked—not the thinnest cover of a soft cloud, not the vaguest hint of a distant cool shower. Send thy angry storm, dark with death, if it is thy wish, and with lashes of lightning startle the sky from end to end.

But call back, my lord, call back this pervading silent heat, still and keen and cruel, burning the heart with dire despair.

Let the cloud of grace bend low from above like the tearful look of the mother on the day of the father's wrath.

Where dost thou stand behind them all, my lover, hiding thyself in the shadows? They push thee and pass thee by on the dusty road, taking thee for naught. I wait here weary hours spreading my offerings for thee, while passers-by come and take my flowers, one by one, and my basket is nearly empty.

The morning time is past, and the noon. In the shade of evening my eyes are drowsy with sleep. Men going home glance at me and smile and fill me with shame. I sit like a beggar maid, drawing my skirt over my face, and when they ask me, what it is I want, I drop my eyes and answer them not. Oh, how, indeed, could I tell them that for thee I wait, and that thou hast promised to come. How could I utter for shame that I keep for my dowry this poverty. Ah, I hug this pride in the secret of my heart. I sit on the grass and gaze upon the sky and dream of the sudden splendour of thy coming—all the lights ablaze, golden pennons flying over thy car, and they at the roadside standing agape, when they see thee come down from thy seat to raise me from the dust, and set at thy side this ragged beggar girl a-tremble with shame and pride, like a creeper in a summer breeze.

But time glides on and still no sound of the wheels of thy chariot. Many a procession passes by with noise and shouts and glamour of glory. Is it only thou who wouldst stand in the shadow silent and behind them all? And only I who would wait and weep and wear out my heart in vain longing?

Early in the day it was whispered that we should sail in a boat, only thou and I, and never a soul in the world would know of this our pilgrimage to no country and to no end.

In that shoreless ocean, at thy silently listening smile my songs would swell in melodies, free as waves, free from all bondage of words.

Is the time not come yet? Are there works still to do? Lo, the evening has come down upon the shore and in the fading light the seabirds come flying to their nests.

Who knows when the chains will be off, and the boat, like the last glimmer of sunset, vanish into the night?

The day was when I did not keep myself in readiness for thee; and entering my heart unbidden even as one of the common crowd, unknown to me, my king, thou didst press the signet of eternity upon many a fleeting moment of my life.

And today when by chance I light upon them and see thy signature, I find they have lain scattered in the dust mixed with the memory of joys and sorrows of my trivial days forgotten.

Thou didst not turn in contempt from my childish play among dust, and the steps that I heard in my playroom are the same that are echoing from star to star.

This is my delight, thus to wait and watch at the wayside where shadow chases light and the rain comes in the wake of the summer.

Messengers, with tidings from unknown skies, greet me

and speed along the road. My heart is glad within, and the breath of the passing breeze is sweet. From dawn till dusk I sit here before my door, and I know that of a sudden the happy moment will arrive when I shall see.

In the meanwhile I smile and I sing all alone. In the meanwhile the air is filling with the perfume of promise.

Have you not heard his silent steps? He comes, comes, ever comes. Every moment and every age, every day and every night he comes, comes, ever comes.

Many a song have I sung in many a mood of mind, but all their notes have always proclaimed, 'He comes, comes, ever comes.' In the fragrant days of sunny April through the forest path he comes, comes, ever comes.

In the rainy gloom of July nights on the thundering chariot of clouds he comes, comes, ever comes.

In sorrow after sorrow it is his steps that press upon my heart, and it is the golden touch of his feet that makes my joy to shine. I know not from what distant time thou art ever coming nearer to meet me. Thy sun and stars can never keep thee hidden from me for aye.

In many a morning and eve thy footsteps have been heard and thy messenger has come within my heart and called me in secret. I know not only why today my life is all astir, and a feeling of tremulous joy is passing through my heart.

It is as if the time were come to wind up my work, and I feel in the air a faint smell of thy sweet presence.

The night is nearly spent waiting for him in vain. I fear lest in the morning he suddenly come to my door when I have fallen asleep wearied out. Oh friends, leave the way open to him—forbid him not. If the sounds of his steps does not wake me, do not try to rouse me, I pray. I wish not to be called from my sleep by the clamorous choir of birds, by the riot of wind at the festival of morning light. Let me sleep undisturbed even if my lord comes of a sudden to my door.

Ah, my sleep, precious sleep, which only waits for his touch to vanish. Ah, my closed eyes that would open their lids only to the light of his smile when he stands before me like a dream emerging from darkness of sleep.

Let him appear before my sight as the first of all lights and all forms. The first thrill of joy to my awakened soul let it come from his glance. And let my return to myself be immediate return to him.

The morning sea of silence broke into ripples of bird songs; and the flowers were all merry by the roadside; and the wealth of gold was scattered through the rift of the clouds while we busily went on our way and paid no heed.

We sang no glad songs nor played; we went not to the village for barter; we spoke not a word nor smiled; we lingered not on the way. We quickened our pace more and more as the time sped by.

The sun rose to the mid sky and doves cooed in the shade. Withered leaves danced and whirled in the hot air of noon. The shepherd boy drowsed and dreamed in the shadow of the banyan tree, and I laid myself down by the water and stretched my tired limbs on the grass.

My companions laughed at me in scorn; they held their heads high and hurried on; they never looked back nor rested; they vanished in the distant blue haze. They crossed many meadows and hills, and passed through strange, far-away countries. All honour to you, heroic host of the interminable path! Mockery and reproach pricked me to rise, but found no response in me. I gave myself up for lost in the depth of a glad humiliation—in the shadow of a dim delight.

The repose of the sun-embroidered green gloom slowly spread over my heart. I forgot for what I had travelled, and I surrendered my mind without struggle to the maze of shadows and songs.

At last, when I woke from my slumber and opened my eyes, I saw thee standing by me, flooding my sleep with thy smile. How I had feared that the path was long and wearisome, and the struggle to reach thee was hard!

You came down from your throne and stood at my cottage door. I was singing all alone in a corner, and the melody caught your ear. You came down and stood at my cottage door.

Masters are many in your hall, and songs are sung there at all hours. But the simple carol of this novice struck at your love. One plaintive little strain mingled with the great music of the world, and with a flower for a prize you came down and stopped at my cottage door.

I had gone a-begging from door to door in the village path, when thy golden chariot appeared in the distance like a gorgeous dream and I wondered who was this King of all kings!

My hopes rose high and methought my evil days were at an end, and I stood waiting for alms to be given unasked and for wealth scattered on all sides in the dust.

The chariot stopped where I stood. Thy glance fell on me and thou camest down with a smile. I felt that the luck of my life had come at last. Then of a sudden thou didst hold out thy right hand and say 'What hast thou to give to me?'

Ah, what a kingly jest was it to open thy palm to a beggar to beg! I was confused and stood undecided, and then from my wallet I slowly took out the least little grain of corn and gave it to thee.

But how great my surprise when at the day's end I emptied my bag on the floor to find a least little gram of gold among the poor heap. I bitterly wept and wished that I had had the heart to give thee my all.

The night darkened. Our day's works had been done. We thought that the last guest had arrived for the night and the doors in the village were all shut. Only some said the king was to come. We laughed and said 'No, it cannot be!'

It seemed there were knocks at the door and we said it was nothing but the wind. We put out the lamps and lay down to sleep. Only some said, 'It is the messenger!' We laughed and said 'No, it must be the wind!'

There came a sound in the dead of the night. We sleepily thought it was the distant thunder. The earth shook, the walls rocked, and it troubled us in our sleep. Only some said it was the sound of wheels. We said in a drowsy murmur, 'No, it must be the rumbling of clouds!'

The night was still dark when the drum sounded. The voice came 'Wake up! delay not!' We pressed our hands on our hearts and shuddered with fear. Some said, 'Lo, there is the king's flag!' We stood up on our feet and cried 'There is no time for delay!' The king has come—but where are lights, where are wreaths? Where is the throne to seat him? Oh, shame! Oh utter shame! Where is th hall, the decorations? Someone has said, 'Vain is this cry! Greet him with empty hands, lead him into thy rooms all bare!'

Open the doors, let the conch-shells be sounded! in the depth of the night has come the king of our dark, dreary house. The thunder roars in the sky. The darkness shudders with lightning. Bring out thy tattered piece of mat and spread it in the courtyard. With the storm has come of a sudden our king of the fearful night.

I thought I should ask of thee—but I dared not—the rose wreath thou hadst on thy neck. Thus I waited for the morning, when thou didst depart, to find a few fragments on the bed. And like a beggar I searched in the dawn only for a stray petal or two.

Ah me, what is it I find? What token left of thy love? It is no flower, no spices, no vase of perfumed water. It is thy mighty sword, flashing as a flame, heavy as a bolt of thunder. The young light of morning comes through the window and spread itself upon thy bed. The morning bird twitters and asks, 'Woman, what hast thou got?' No, it is no flower, nor spices, nor vase of perfumed water—it is thy dreadful sword.

I sit and muse in wonder, what gift is this of thine. I can find no place to hide it. I am ashamed to wear it, frail as I am, and it hurts me when press it to my bosom. Yet shall I bear in my heart this honour of the burden of pain, this gift of thine.

From now there shall be no fear left for me in this world, and thou shalt be victorious in all my strife. Thou hast left death for my companion and I shall crown him with my life. Thy sword is with me to cut asunder my bonds, and there shall be no fear left for me in the world.

From now I leave off all petty decorations. Lord of my heart, no more shall there be for me waiting and weeping in corners, no more coyness and sweetness of demeanour. Thou hast given me thy sword for adornment. No more doll's decorations for me!

Beautiful is thy wristlet, decked with stars and cunningly wrought in myriad-coloured jewels. But more beautiful to me thy sword with its curve of lightning like the outspread wings of the divine bird of Vishnu, perfectly poised in the angry red light of the sunset.

It quivers like the one last response of life in ecstasy of pain at the final stroke of death; it shines like the pure flame of being burning up earthly sense with one fierce flash.

Beautiful is thy wristlet, decked with starry gems; but thy sword, O lord of thunder, is wrought with uttermost beauty, terrible to behold or think of.

I asked nothing from thee; I uttered not my name to thine ear. When thou took'st thy leave I stood silent. I was alone by the well where the shadow of the tree fell aslant, and the women had gone home with their brown earthen pitchers full to the brim. They called me and shouted, 'Come with us, the morning is wearing on to noon.' But I languidly lingered awhile lost in the midst of vague musings.

I heard not thy steps as thou camest. Thine eyes were sad when they fell on me; thy voice was tired as thou spokest low—'Ah, I am a thirsty traveller.' I started up from my day-dreams and poured water from my jar on thy joined palms. The leaves rustled overhead; the cuckoo sang from the unseen dark, and perfume of *babla* flowers came from the bend of the road.

I stood speechless with shame when my name thou didst ask. Indeed, what had I done for thee to keep me in remembrance? But the memory that I could give water to thee to allay thy thirst will cling to my heart and enfold it in sweetness. The morning hour is late, the bird sings in weary notes, *neem* leaves rustle overhead and I sit and think and think. Languor is upon your heart and the slumber is still on your eyes. Has not the word come to you that the flower is reigning in splendour among thorns? Wake, oh awaken! let not the time pass in vain!

At the end of the stony path, in the country of virgin solitude, my friend is sitting all alone. Deceive him not. Wake, oh awaken!

What if the sky pants and trembles with the heat of the

midday sun—what if the burning sand spreads its mantle of thirst—Is there no joy in the deep of your heart? At every footfall of yours, will not the harp of the road break out in sweet music of pain?

Thus it is that thy joy in me is so full. Thus it is that thou hast come down to me. O thou lord of all heavens, where would be thy love if I were not?

Thou hast taken me as thy partner of all this wealth. In my heart is the endless play of thy delight. In my life thy will is ever taking shape.

And for this, thou who art the King of kings hast decked thyself in beauty to captivate my heart. And for this thy love loses itself in the love of thy lover, and there art thou seen in the perfect union of two.

Light, my light, the world-filling light, the eye-kissing light, heart-sweetening light!

Ah, the light dances, my darling, at the centre of my life; the light strikes, my darling, the chords of my love; the sky opens, the wind runs wild, laughter passes over the earth.

The butterflies spread their sails on the sea of light. Lilies and jasmines surge up on the crest of the waves of light.

The light is shattered into gold on every cloud, my darling, and it scatters gems in profusion.

Mirth spreads from leaf to leaf, my darling, and gladness without measure. The heaven's river has drowned its banks and the flood of joy is abroad.

Let all the strains of joy mingle in my last song—the joy that makes the earth flow over in the riotous excess of the grass, the joy that sets the twin brothers, life and death, dancing over the wide world, the joy that sweeps in with the tempest, shaking and waking all life with laughter, the joy that sits still with its tears on the open red lotus of pain, and the joy that throws everything it has upon the dust, and knows not a word.

Yes, I know, this is nothing but thy love, O beloved of my heart—this golden light that dances upon the leaves, these idle clouds sailing across the sky, this passing breeze leaving its coolness upon my forehead.

The morning light has flooded my eyes—this is thy

message to my heart. Thy face is bent from above, thy eyes look down on my eyes, and my heart has touched thy feet.

On the seashore of endless worlds children meet. The infinite sky is motionless overhead and the restless water is boisterous. On the seashore of endless worlds the children meet with shouts and dances.

They build their houses with sand and they play with empty shells. With withered leaves they weave their boats and smilingly float them on the vast deep. Children have their play on the seashore of worlds.

They know not how to swim, they know not how to cast nets. Pearl fishers dive for pearls, merchants sail in their ships, while children gather pebbles and scatter them again. they seek not for hidden treasures, they know not how to cast nets.

The sea surges up with laughter and pale gleams the smile of the sea beach. Death-dealing waves sing meaningless ballads to the children, even like a mother while rocking her baby's cradle. The sea plays with children, and pale gleams the smile of the sea beach.

On the seashore of endless worlds children meet. Tempest roams in the pathless sky, ships get wrecked in the trackless water, death is abroad and children play. On the seashore of endless worlds is the great meeting of children.

The sleep that flits on baby's eyes—does anybody know from where it comes? Yes, there is a rumour that it has its dwelling where, in the fairy village among shadows of the forest dimly lit with glow-worms, there hang two timid buds of enchantment. From there it comes to kiss baby's eyes.

The smile that flickers on baby's lips when he sleeps—does anybody know where it was born? Yes, there is a rumour that a young pale beam of a crescent moon touched the edge of a vanishing autumn cloud, and there the smile was first born in the dream of a dew-washed morning—the smile that flickers on baby's lips when he sleeps.

The sweet, soft freshness that blooms on baby's limbs—does anybody know where it was hidden so long? Yes, when the mother was a young girl it lay pervading her heart in tender and silent mystery of love—the sweet, soft freshness that has bloomed on baby's limbs. When I bring to you coloured toys, my child, I understand why there is such a play of colours on clouds, on water, and why flowers are painted in tints—when I give coloured toys to you, my child.

When I sing to make you dance I truly now why there is music in leaves, and why waves send their chorus of voices to the heart of the listening earth—when I sing to make you dance.

When I bring sweet things to your greedy hands I know why there is honey in the cup of the flowers and why fruits are secretly filled with sweet juice—when I bring sweet things to your greedy hands.

When I kiss your face to make you smile, my darling, I surely understand what pleasure streams from the sky in morning light, and what delight that is that is which the summer breeze brings to my body—when I kiss you to make you smile.

Thou hast made me known to friends whom I knew not. Thou hast given me seats in homes not my own. Thou hast brought the distant near and made a brother of the stranger.

I am uneasy at heart when I have to leave my accustomed shelter; I forget that there abides the old in the new, and that there also thou abidest.

Through birth and death, in this world or in others, wherever thou leadest me it is thou, the same, the one companion of my endless life who ever linkest my heart with bonds of joy to the unfamiliar.

When one knows thee, then alien there is none, then no door is shut. Oh, grant me my prayer that I may never lose the bliss of the touch of the one in the play of many.

On the slope of the desolate river among tall grasses I asked her, 'Maiden, where do you go shading your lamp with your mantle? My house is all dark and lonesome—lend me your light!' she raised her dark eyes for a moment and looked at my face through the dusk. 'I have come to the river,' she said, 'to float my lamp on the stream when the daylight wanes in the west.' I stood alone among tall grasses and watched the timid flame of her lamp uselessly drifting in the tide.

In the silence of gathering night I asked her, 'Maiden, your lights are all lit—then where do you go with your lamp? My house is all dark and lonesome—lend me your light.' She raised her dark eyes on my face and stood for a moment doubtful. 'I have come,' she said at last, 'to dedicate my lamp to the sky.' I stood and watched her light uselessly burning in the void.

In the moonless gloom of midnight I ask her, 'Maiden, what is your quest, holding the lamp near your heart? My house is all dark and lonesome—lend me your light.' She stopped for a minute and thought and gazed at my face in the dark. 'I have brought my light,' she said, 'to join the carnival of lamps.' I stood and watched her little lamp uselessly lost among lights.

What divine drink wouldst thou have, my God, from this overflowing cup of my life?

My poet, is it thy delight to see thy creation through my eyes and to stand at the portals of my ears silently to listen to thine own eternal harmony?

Thy world is weaving words in my mind and thy joy is adding music to them. Thou givest thyself to me in love and then feelest thine own entire sweetness in me.

She who ever had remained in the depth of my being, in the twilight of gleams and of glimpses; she who never opened her veils in the morning light, will be my last gift to thee, my God, folded in my final song.

Words have wooed yet failed to win her; persuasion has stretched to her its eager arms in vain.

I have roamed from country to country keeping her in the core of my heart, and around her have risen and fallen the growth and decay of my life.

Over my thoughts and actions, my slumbers and dreams, she reigned yet dwelled alone and apart.

many a man knocked at my door and asked for her and turned away in despair.

There was none in the world who ever saw her face to face, and she remained in her loneliness waiting for thy recognition.

Thou art the sky and thou art the nest as well. O thou beautiful, there in the nest is thy love that encloses the soul with colours and sounds and odours. There comes the morning with the golden basket in her right hand bearing the wreath of beauty, silently to crown the earth.

And there comes the evening over the lonely meadows deserted by herds, through trackless paths, carrying cool draughts of peace in her golden pitcher from the western ocean of rest. But there, where spreads the infinite sky for the soul to take her flight in, reigns the stainless white radiance. There is no day nor night, nor form nor colour, and never, never a word.

Thy sunbeam comes upon this earth of mine with arms outstretched and stands at my door the livelong day to carry back to thy feet clouds made of my tears and sighs and songs.

With fond delight thou wrappest about thy starry breast that mantle of misty cloud, turning it into numberless shapes and folds and colouring it with hues everchanging.

It is so light and so fleeting, tender and tearful and dark, that is why thou lovest it, O thou spotless and serene. And that is why it may cover thy awful white light with its pathetic shadows.

The same stream of life that runs through my veins night and day runs through the world and dances in rhythmic measures. It is the same life that shoots in joy through the dust of the earth in numberless blades of grass and breaks into tumultuous waves of leaves and flowers.

It is the same life that is rocked in the ocean-cradle of birth and of death, in ebb and in flow. I feel my limbs are made glorious by the touch of this world of life. And my pride is from the life-throb of ages dancing in my blood this moment.

Is it beyond thee to be glad with the gladness of this rhythm? to be tossed and lost and broken in the whirl of this fearful joy? All things rush on, they stop not, they look not behind, no power can hold them back, they rush on.

Keeping steps with that restless, rapid music, seasons come dancing and pass away—colours, tunes, and perfumes pour in endless cascades in the abounding joy that scatters and gives up and dies every moment. That I should make much of myself and turn it on all sides, thus casting coloured shadows on thy radiance—such is thy *maya.* Thou settest a barrier in thine own being and then callest thy severed self in myriad notes. This thy self-separation has taken body in me.

The poignant song is echoed through all the sky in many-coloured tears and smiles, alarms and hopes; waves rise up and sink again, dreams break and form. In me is thy own defeat of self.

This screen that thou hast raised is painted with innumerable figures with the brush of the night and the day. Behind it thy seat is woven in wondrous mysteries of curves, casting away all barren lines of straightness. The great pageant of thee and me has overspread the sky. With the tune of thee and me all the air is vibrant, and all ages pass with the hiding and seeking of thee and me.

He it is, the innermost one, who awakens my being with his deep hidden touches. He it is who puts his enchantment upon these eyes and joyfully plays on the chords of my heart in varied cadence of pleasure and pain.

He it is who weaves the web of this *maya* in evanescent hues of gold and silver, blue and green, and lets peep out through the folds his feet, at whose touch I forget myself.

Days come and ages pass, and it is ever he who moves my heart in many a name, in many a guise, in many a rapture of joy and of sorrow. Deliverance is not for me in renunciation. I feel the embrace of freedom in a thousand bonds of delight.

Thou ever pourest for me the fresh draught of thy wine of various colours and fragrance, filling this earthen vessel to the brim. My world will light its hundred different lamps with thy flame and place them before the altar of thy temple.

No, I will never shut the doors of my senses. The delights of sight and hearing and touch will bear thy delight. Yes, all my illusions will burn into illumination of joy, and all my desires ripen into fruits of love. The day is no more, the shadow is upon the earth. It is time that I go to the stream to fill my pitcher. The evening air is eager with the sad music of the water. Ah, it calls me out into the dusk. In the lonely lane there is no passer-by, the wind is up, the ripples are rampant in the river. I know not if I shall come back home. I know not whom I shall chance to meet. There at the fording in the little boat the unknown man plays upon his lute.

Thy gifts to us mortals fulfil all our needs and yet run back to thee undiminished. The river has its everyday work to do and hastens through fields and hamlets; yet its incessant stream winds towards the washing of thy feet.

The flower sweetens the air with its perfume; yet its last service is to offer itself to thee. Thy worship does not impoverish the world.

From the words of the poet men take what meanings please them; yet their last meaning points to thee. Day after day, O lord of my life, shall I stand before thee face to face. With folded hands, O lord of all worlds, shall I stand before thee face to face.

Under thy great sky in solitude and silence, with humble heart shall I stand before thee face to face. In this laborious world of thine, tumultuous with toil and with struggle, among hurrying crowds shall I stand before thee face to face.

And when my work shall be done in this world, O King of kings, alone and speechless shall I stand before thee face to face. I know thee as my God and stand apart—I do not know thee as my own and come closer. I know thee as my father and bow before thy feet—I do not grasp thy hand as my friend's.

I stand not where thou comest down and ownest thyself as mine, there to clasp thee to my heart and take thee as my comrade. Thou art the Brother amongst my brothers, but I heed them not, I divide not my earnings with them, thus sharing my all with thee.

In pleasure and in pain I stand not by the side of men, and thus stand by thee. I shrink to give up my life, and thus do not plunge into the great waters of life.

When the creation was new and all the stars shone in their first splendour, the gods held their assembly in the sky and sang 'Oh, the picture of perfection! the joy unalloyed!'

But one cried of a sudden—'It seems that somewhere there

is a break in the chain of light and one of the stars has been lost.' The golden string of their harp snapped, their song stopped, and they cried in dismay—'Yes, that lost star was the best, she was the glory of all heavens!'

From that day the search is unceasing for her, and the cry goes on from one to the other that in her the world has lost its one joy! Only in the deepest silence of night the stars smile and whisper among themselves—'Vain is this seeking! unbroken perfection is over all!'

If it is not my portion to meet thee in this life then let me ever feel that I have missed thy sight—let me not forget for a moment, let me carry the pangs of this sorrow in my dreams and in my wakeful hours.

As my days pass in the crowded market of this world and my hands grow full with the daily profits, let me ever feel that I have gained nothing—let me not forget for a moment, let me carry the pangs of this sorrow in my dreams and in my wakeful hours.

When I sit by the roadside, tired and panting, when I spread my bed low in the dust, let me ever feel that the long journey is still before me—let me not forget a moment, let me carry the pangs of this sorrow in my dreams and in my wakeful hours.

When my rooms have been decked out and the flutes sound and the laughter there is loud, let me ever feel that I have not invited thee to my house—let me not forget for a moment, let me carry the pangs of this sorrow in my dreams and in my wakeful hours.

I am like a remnant of a cloud of autumn uselessly roaming in the sky, O my sun ever-glorious! Thy touch has not yet melted my vapour, making me one with thy light, and thus I count months and years separated from thee.

If this be thy wish and if this be thy play, then take this fleeting emptiness of mine, paint it with colours, gild it with gold, float it on the wanton wind and spread it in varied wonders.

And again when it shall be thy wish to end this play at night, I shall melt and vanish away in the dark, or it may be in a smile of the white morning, in a coolness of purity transparent. On many an idle day have I grieved over lost time. But it is never lost, my lord. Thou hast taken every moment of my life in thine own hands.

Hidden in the heart of things thou art nourishing seeds into sprouts, buds into blossoms, and ripening flowers into fruitfulness. I was tired and sleeping on my idle bed and imagined all work had ceased. In the morning I woke up and found my garden full with wonders of flowers. Time is endless in thy hands, my lord. There is none to count thy minutes. Days and nights pass and ages bloom and fade like flowers. Thou knowest how to wait.

Thy centuries follow each other perfecting a small wild flower. We have no time to lose, and having no time we must scramble for a chances. We are too poor to be late.

And thus it is that time goes by while I give it to every querulous man who claims it, and thine altar is empty of all offerings to the last. At the end of the day I hasten in fear lest thy gate to be shut; but I find that yet there is time.

Mother, I shall weave a chain of pearls for thy neck with my tears of sorrow.

The stars have wrought their anklets of light to deck thy feet, but mine will hang upon thy breast.

Wealth and fame come from thee and it is for thee to give or to withhold them. But this my sorrow is absolutely mine own, and when I bring it to thee as my offering thou rewardest me with thy grace.

It is the pang of separation that spreads throughout the world and gives birth to shapes innumerable in the infinite sky. It is this sorrow of separation that gazes in silence all nights from star to star and becomes lyric among rustling leaves in rainy darkness of July.

It is this overspreading pain that deepens into loves and desires, into sufferings and joy in human homes; and this it is that ever melts and flows in songs through my poet's heart.

When the warriors came out first from their master's hall, where had they hid their power? Where were their armour and their arms?

They looked poor and helpless, and the arrows were showered upon them on the day they came out from their master's hall.

When the warriors marched back again to their master's hall where did they hide their power?

They had dropped the sword and dropped the bow and the arrow; peace was on their foreheads, and they had left the fruits of their life behind them on the day they marched back again to their master's hall.

Death, thy servant, is at my door. He has crossed the unknown sea and brought thy call to my home.

The night is dark and my heart is fearful—yet I will take up the lamp, open my gates and bow to him my welcome. It is thy messenger who stands at my door.

I will worship him placing at his feet the treasure of my heart. He will go back with his errand done, leaving a dark shadow on my morning; and in my desolate home only my forlorn self will remain as my last offering to thee.

In desperate hope I go and search for her in all the corners of my room; I find her not.

My house is small and what once has gone from it can never be regained. But infinite is thy mansion, my lord, and seeking her I have to come to thy door.

I stand under the golden canopy of thine evening sky and I lift my eager eyes to thy face.

I have come to the brink of eternity from which nothing can vanish—no hope, no happiness, no vision of a face seen through tears.

Oh, dip my emptied life into that ocean, plunge it into the deepest fullness. Let me for once feel that lost sweet touch in the allness of the universe.

Deity of the ruined temple! The broken strings of *Vina* sing no more your praise. The bells in the evening proclaim not your time of worship. The air is still and silent about you.

In your desolate dwelling comes the vagrant spring breeze. It brings the tidings of flowers—the flowers that for your worship are offered no more.

Your worshipper of old wanders ever longing for favour

still refused. In the eventide, when fires and shadows mingle with the gloom of dust, he wearily comes back to the ruined temple with hunger in his heart.

Many a festival day comes to you in silence, deity of the ruined temple. Many a night of worship goes away with lamp unlit. Many new images are built by masters of cunning art and carried to the holy stream of oblivion when their time is come. Only the deity of the ruined temple remains unworshipped in deathless neglect.

No more noisy, loud words from me—such is my master's will. Henceforth I deal in whispers. The speech of my heart will be carried on in murmurings of a song.

Men hasten to the King's market. All the buyers and sellers are there. But I have my untimely leave in the middle of the day, in the thick of work.

Let then the flowers come out in my garden, though it is not their time; and let the midday bees strike up their lazy hum. Full many an hour have I spent in the strife of the good and the evil, but now it is the pleasure of my playmate of the empty days to draw my heart on to him; and I know not why is this sudden call to what useless inconsequence!

On the day when death will knock at thy door what wilt thou offer to him? Oh, I will set before my guest the full vessel of my life—I will never let him go with empty hands.

All the sweet vintage of all my autumn days and summer nights, all the earnings and gleanings of my busy life will I place before him at the close of my days when death will knock at my door. O thou the last fulfilment of life, Death, my death, come and whisper to me!

Day after day I have kept watch for thee; for thee have I borne the joys and pangs of life. All that I am, that I have, that I hope and all my love have ever flowed towards thee in depth of secrecy. One final glance from thine eyes and my life will be ever thine own.

The flowers have been woven and the garland is ready for the bridegroom. After the wedding the bride shall leave her home and meet her lord alone in the solitude of night.

I know that the day will come when my sight of this earth

shall be lost, and life will take its leave in silence, drawing the last curtain over my eyes.

Yet stars will watch at night, and morning rise as before, and hours heave like sea waves casting up pleasures and pains.

When I think of this end of my moments, the barrier of the moments breaks and I see by the light of death thy world with its careless treasures. Rare is its lowliest seat, rare is its meanest of lives.

Things that I longed for in vain and things that I got—let them pass. Let me but truly possess the things that I ever spurned and overlooked. I have got my leave. Bid me farewell, my brothers! I bow to you all and take my departure.

Here I give back the keys of my door—and I give up all claims to my house. I only ask for last kind words from you. We were neighbours for long, but I received more than I could give. Now the day has dawned and the lamp that lit my dark corner is out. A summons has come and I am ready for my journey. At this time of my parting, wish me good luck, my friends! The sky is flushed with the dawn and my path lies beautiful. Ask not what I have with me to take there. I start on my journey with empty hands and expectant heart.

I shall put on my wedding garland. Mine is not the red-brown dress of the traveller, and though there are dangers on the way I have no fear in mind. The evening star will come out when my voyage is done and the plaintive notes of the twilight melodies be struck up from the King's gateway.

I was not aware of the moment when I first crossed the threshold of this life. What was the power that made me open out into this vast mystery like a bud in the forest at midnight!

When in the morning I looked upon the light I felt in a moment that I was no stranger in this world, that the inscrutable without name and form had taken me in its arms in the form of my own mother.

Even so, in death the same unknown will appear as ever known to me. And because I love this life, I know I shall love death as well.

The child cries out when from the right breast the mother takes it away, in the very next moment to find in the left one its consolation. When I go from hence let this be my parting word, that what I have seen is unsurpassable. I have tasted of the hidden honey of this lotus that expands on the ocean of light, and thus am I blessed—let this be my parting word.

In this playhouse of infinite forms I have had my play and here have I caught sight of him that is formless. My whole body and my limbs have thrilled with his touch who is beyond touch; and if the end comes here, let it come—let this be my parting word.

When my play was with thee I never questioned who thou wert. I knew nor shyness nor fear, my life was boisterous. In the early morning thou wouldst call me from my sleep like my own comrade and lead me running from glade to glade.

On those days I never cared to know the meaning of songs thou sangest to me. Only my voice took up the tunes, and my heart danced in their cadence. Now, when the playtime is over, what is this sudden sight that is come upon me? The world with eyes bent upon thy feet stands in awe with all its silent stars. I will deck thee with trophies, garlands of my defeat. It is never in my power to escape unconquered. I surely know my pride will go to the wall, my life will burst its bonds in exceeding pain, and my empty heart will sob out in music like a hollow reed, and the stone will melt in tears.

I surely know the hundred petals of a lotus will not remain closed for ever and the secret recess of its honey will be bared. From the blue sky an eye shall gaze upon me and summon me in silence. Nothing will be left for me, nothing whatever, and utter death shall I receive at thy feet. When I give up the helm I know that the time has come for thee to take it. What there is to do will be instantly done. Vain is this struggle. Then take away your hands and silently put up with your defeat, my heart, and think it your good fortune to sit perfectly still where you are placed. These my lamps are blown out at every little puff of wind, and trying to light them I forget all else again and again. But I shall be wise this time and wait in the dark, spreading my mat on the floor; and whenever it is thy pleasure, my lord, come silently and take thy seat here.

I dive down into the depth of the ocean of forms, hoping

to gain the perfect pearl of the formless. No more sailing from harbour to harbour with this my weather-beaten boat. The days are long passed when my sport was to be tossed on waves. And now I am eager to die into the deathless. Into the audience hall by the fathomless abyss where swells up the music of toneless strings I shall take this harp of my life.

I shall tune it to the notes of forever, and when it has sobbed out its last utterance, lay down my silent harp at the feet of the silent. Ever in my life have I sought thee with my songs. It was they who led me from door to door, and with them have I felt about me, searching and touching my world.

It was my songs that taught me all the lessons I ever learnt; they showed me secret paths, they brought before my sight many a star on the horizon of my heart.

They guided me all the day long to the mysteries of the country of pleasure and pain, and, at last, to what palace gate have the brought me in the evening at the end of my journey? I boasted among men that I had known you. They see your pictures in all works of mine. They come and ask me, 'Who is he?' I know not how to answer them. I say, 'Indeed, I cannot tell.' They blame me and they go away in scorn. And you sit there smiling.

I put my tales of you into lasting songs. The secret gushes out from my heart. They come and ask me, 'Tell me all your meanings.' I know not how to answer them. I say, 'Ah, who knows what they mean!' They smile and go away in utter scorn. And you sit there smiling. In one salutation to thee, my God, let all my senses spread out and touch this world at thy feet. Like a rain-cloud of July hung low with its burden of unshed showers let all my mind bend down at thy door in one salutation to thee. Let all my songs gather together their diverse strains into a single current and flow to a sea of silence in one salutation to thee.

Like a flock of homesick cranes flying night and day back to their mountain nests let all my life take its voyage to its eternal home in one salutation to thee.

Chapter 6

Text

GITANJALI
"Song Offerings"

Mind Without Fear

Where the mind is without fear and the head is held high;
Where knowledge is free;
Where the world has not been broken up into fragments by narrow domestic walls;
Where words come out from the depth of truth;
Where tireless striving stretches its arms towards perfection;
Where the clear stream of reason has not lost its way into the dreary desert sand of dead habit;
Where the mind is led forward by thee into ever-widening thought and action—Into that heaven of freedom, my Father, let my country awake.

Little Flute

Thou hast made me endless, such is thy pleasure. This frail vessel thou emptiest again and again, and fillest it ever with fresh life. This little flute of a reed thou hast carried over hills and dales, and hast breathed through it melodies eternally new.

At the immortal touch of thy hands my little heart loses its limits in joy and gives birth to utterance ineffable. Thy infinite gifts come to me only on these very small hands of mine. Ages pass, and still thou pourest, and still there is room to fill.

Purity

Life of my life, I shall ever try to keep my body pure, knowing that thy living touch is upon all my limbs. I shall ever try to keep all untruths out from my thoughts, knowing that thou art that truth which has kindled the light of reason in my mind. I shall ever try to drive all evils away from my heart and keep my love in flower, knowing that thou hast thy seat in the inmost shrine of my heart. And it shall be my endeavour to reveal thee in my actions, knowing it is thy power gives me strength to act.

Moment's Indulgence

I ask for a moment's indulgence to sit by thy side. The works that I have in hand I will finish afterwards. Away from the sight of thy face my heart knows no rest nor respite, and my work becomes an endless toil in a shoreless sea of toil. Today the summer has come at my window with its sighs and murmurs; and the bees are plying their minstrelsy at the court of the flowering grove. Now it is time to sit quite, face to face with thee, and to sing dedication of life in this silent and overflowing leisure.

Flower

Pluck this little flower and take it, delay not! I fear lest it droop and drop into the dust. I may not find a place in thy garland, but honour it with a touch of pain from thy hand and pluck it. I fear lest the day end before I am aware, and the time of offering go by. Though its colour be not deep and its smell be faint, use this flower in thy service and pluck it while there is time.

Fool

O Fool, try to carry thyself upon thy own shoulders! O beggar, to come beg at thy own door! Leave all thy burdens on his hands who can bear all, and never look behind in regret. Thy desire at once puts out the light from the lamp it touches with its breath. It is unholy—take not thy gifts through its unclean hands. Accept only what is offered by sacred love.

Leave This

Leave this chanting and singing and telling of beads!

Whom dost thou worship in this lonely dark corner of a temple with doors all shut?

Open thine eyes and see thy God is not before thee!

He is there where the tiller is tilling the hard ground and where the pathmaker is breaking stones.

He is with them in sun and in shower, and his garment is covered with dust.

Put off thy holy mantle and even like him come down on the dusty soil!

Deliverance?

Where is this deliverance to be found?

Our master himself has joyfully taken upon nim the bonds of creation; he is bound with us all for ever.

Come out of thy meditations and leave aside thy flowers and incense!

What harm is there if thy clothes become tattered and stained? Meet him and stand by him in toil and in sweat of thy brow.

Journey Home

The time that my journey takes is long and the way of it long. I came out on the chariot of the first gleam of light, and pursued my voyage through the wildernesses of worlds leaving my track on many a star and planet.

It is the most distant course that comes nearest to thyself, and that training is the most intricate which leads to the utter simplicity of a tune.

The traveller has to knock at every alien door to come to his own, and one has to wander through all the outer worlds to reach the innermost shrine at the end.

My eyes strayed far and wide before I shut them and said 'Here art thou!'

The question and the cry 'Oh, where?' melt into tears of a thousand streams and deluge the world with the flood of the assurance 'I am!'

Song Unsung

The song that I came to sing remains unsung to this day.

I have spent my days in stringing and in unstringing my instrument.

The time has not come true, the words have not been rightly set; only there is the agony of wishing in my heart.

The blossom has not opened; only the wind is sighing by.

I have not seen his face, nor have I listened to his voice; only I have heard his gentle footsteps from the road before my house.

The livelong day has passed in spreading his seat on the floor; but the lamp has not been lit and I cannot ask him into my house. I live in the hope of meeting with him; but this meeting is not yet.

Strong Mercy

My desires are many and my cry is pitiful, but ever didst thou save me by hard refusals; and this strong mercy has been wrought into my life through and through.

Day by day thou art making me worthy of the simple, great gifts that thou gavest to me unasked—this sky and the light, this body and the life and the mind—saving me from perils of overmuch desire.

There are times when I languidly linger and times when I awaken and hurry in search of my goal; but cruelly thou hidest thyself from before me.

Day by day thou art making me worthy of thy full acceptance by refusing me ever and anon, saving me from perils of weak, uncertain desire.

Patience

If thou speakest not I will fill my heart with thy silence and endure it. I will keep still and wait like the night with starry vigil and its head bent low with patience.

The morning will surely come, the darkness will vanish, and thy voice pour down in golden streams breaking through the sky. Then thy words will take wing in songs from every one of my birds' nests, and thy melodies will break forth in flowers in all my forest groves.

Lotus

On the day when the lotus bloomed, alas, my mind was straying, and I knew it not. My basket was empty and the flower remained unheeded.

Only now and again a sadness fell upon me, and I started up from my dream and felt a sweet trace of a strange fragrance in the south wind.

That vague sweetness made my heart ache with longing and it seemed to me that is was the eager breath of the summer seeking for its completion.

I knew not then that it was so near, that it was mine, and that this perfect sweetness had blossomed in the depth of my own heart.

Boat

I must launch out my boat.

The languid hours pass by on the shore—Alas for me!

The spring has done its flowering and taken leave.

And now with the burden of faded futile flowers I wait and linger.

The waves have become clamorous, and upon the bank in the shady lane the yellow leaves flutter and fall.

What emptiness do you gaze upon!

Do you not feel a thrill passing through the air with the notes of the far-away song floating from the other shore?

Friend

Art thou abroad on this stormy night on thy journey of love, my friend?

The sky groans like one in despair.

I have no sleep tonight.

Ever and again I open my door and look out on the darkness, my friend! I can see nothing before me. I wonder where lies thy path!

By what dim shore of the ink-black river, by what far edge of the frowning forest, through what mazy depth of gloom art thou threading thy course to come to me, my friend?

When Day Is Done

If the day is done, if birds sing no more, if the wind has flagged tired, then draw the veil of darkness thick upon me, even as thou hast wrapt the earth with the coverlet of sleep and tenderly closed the petals of the drooping lotus at dusk.

From the traveller, whose sack of provisions is empty before the voyage is ended, whose garment is torn and dust-laden, whose strength is exhausted, remove shame and poverty, and renew his life like a flower under the cover of thy kindly night.

Sleep

In the night of weariness
let me give myself up to sleep without struggle, resting my trust upon thee.

Let me not force my flagging spirit into a poor preparation for thy worship.

It is thou who drawest the veil of night upon the tired eyes of the day to renew its sight in a fresher gladness of awakening.

Lamp of Love

Light, oh where is the light?

Kindle it with the burning fire of desire!

There is the lamp but never a flicker of a flame—is such thy fate, my heart?

Ah, death were better by far for thee!

Misery knocks at thy door, and her message is that thy lord is wakeful, and he calls thee to the love-tryst through the darkness of night.

The sky is overcast with clouds and the rain is ceaseless.

I know not what this is that stirs in me—

I know not its meaning.

A moment's flash of lightning drags down a deeper gloom

on my sight, and my heart gropes for the path to where the music of the night calls me.

Light, oh where is the light!

Kindle it with the burning fire of desire!

It thunders and the wind rushes screaming through the void.

The night is black as a black stone.

Let not the hours pass by in the dark.

Kindle the lamp of love with thy life.

Dungeon

He whom I enclose with my name is weeping in this dungeon.

I am ever busy building this wall all around; and as this wall goes up into the sky day by day I lose sight of my true being in its dark shadow.

I take pride in this great wall, and I plaster it with dust and sand lest a least hole should be left in this name; and for all the care I take I lose sight of my true being.

Who is This?

I came out alone on my way to my tryst.
But who is this that follows me in the silent dark?
I move aside to avoid his presence but I escape him not.
He makes the dust rise from the earth with his swagger;
he adds his loud voice to every word that I utter.
He is my own little self, my lord, he knows no shame;
but I am ashamed to come to thy door in his company.

Prisoner

'Prisoner, tell me, who was it that bound you?'

'It was my master,' said the prisoner.

'I thought I could outdo everybody in the world in wealth and power, and I amassed in my own treasure-house the money due to my king.

When sleep overcame me I lay upon the bed that was for my lord, and on waking up I found I was a prisoner in my own treasure-house.' 'Prisoner, tell me, who was it that wrought this unbreakable chain?' 'It was I,' said the prisoner, 'who forged this chain very carefully. I thought my invincible power would hold the world captive

leaving me in a freedom undisturbed.
Thus night and day I worked at the chain
with huge fires and cruel hard strokes.
When at last the work was done
and the links were complete and unbreakable,
I found that it held me in its grip.'

Free Love

By all means they try to hold me secure who love me in this world. But it is otherwise with thy love which is greater than theirs, and thou keepest me free.

Lest I forget them they never venture to leave me alone.

But day passes by after day and thou art not seen.

If I call not thee in my prayers, if I keep not thee in my heart, thy love for me still waits for my love.

Little of Me

Let only that little be left of me whereby I may name thee my all.

Let only that little be left of my will whereby I may feel thee on every side, and come to thee in everything, and offer to thee my love every moment.

Let only that little be left of me whereby I may never hide thee.

Let only that little of my fetters be left whereby I am bound with thy will, and thy purpose is carried out in my life—and that is the fetter of thy love.

Give Me Strength

This is my prayer to thee, my lord—strike, strike at the root of penury in my heart.

Give me the strength lightly to bear my joys and sorrows.

Give me the strength to make my love fruitful in service.

Give me the strength never to disown the poor or bend my knees before insolent might.

Give me the strength to raise my mind high above daily trifles.

And give me the strength to surrender my strength to thy will with love.

Closed Path

I thought that my voyage had come to its end at the last limit of my power,—that the path before me was closed, that provisions were exhausted and the time come to take shelter in a silent obscurity.

But I find that thy will knows no end in me.

And when old words die out on the tongue, new melodies break forth from the heart; and where the old tracks are lost, new country is revealed with its wonders.

Only Thee

That I want thee, only thee—let my heart repeat without end.

All desires that distract me, day and night, are false and empty to the core. As the night keeps hidden in its gloom the petition for light, even thus in the depth of my unconsciousness rings the cry —'I want thee, only thee'.

As the storm still seeks its end in peace when it strikes against peace with all its might, even thus my rebellion strikes against thy love and still its cry is —'I want thee, only thee'.

Beggarly Heart

When the heart is hard and parched up, come upon me with a shower of mercy.

When grace is lost from life, come with a burst of song.

When tumultuous work raises its din on all sides shutting me out from beyond, come to me, my lord of silence, with thy peace and rest.

When my beggarly heart sits crouched, shut up in a corner, break open the door, my king, and come with the ceremony of a king. When desire blinds the mind with delusion and dust, O thou holy one, thou wakeful, come with thy light and thy thunder.

Sail Away

Early in the day it was whispered that we should sail in a boat, only thou and I, and never a soul in the world would know of this our pilgrimage to no country and to no end.

In that shoreless ocean, at thy silently listening smile my songs would swell in melodies, free as waves, free from all bondage of words.

Is the time not come yet?

Are there works still to do?

Lo, the evening has come down upon the shore and in the fading light the seabirds come flying to their nests.

Who knows when the chains will be off, and the boat, like the last glimmer of sunset, vanish into the night?

Signet of Eternity

The day was when I did not keep myself in readiness for thee; and entering my heart unbidden even as one of the common crowd, unknown to me, my king, thou didst press the signet of eternity upon many a fleeting moment of my life.

And today when by chance I light upon them and see thy signature, I find they have lain scattered in the dust mixed with the memory of joys and sorrows of my trivial days forgotten.

Thou didst not turn in contempt from my childish play among dust, and the steps that I heard in my playroom are the same that are echoing from star to star.

Where Shadow Chases Light

This is my delight, thus to wait and watch at the wayside where shadow chases light and the rain comes in the wake of the summer.

Messengers, with tidings from unknown skies, greet me and speed along the road.

My heart is glad within, and the breath of the passing breeze is sweet.

From dawn till dusk I sit here before my door, and I know that of a sudden the happy moment will arrive when I shall see.

In the meanwhile I smile and I sing all alone.

In the meanwhile the air is filling with the perfume of promise.

Silent Steps

Have you not heard his silent steps?

He comes, comes, ever comes.

Every moment and every age, every day and every night he comes, comes, ever comes.

Many a song have I sung in many a mood of mind, but all their notes have always proclaimed,

'He comes, comes, ever comes.'

In the fragrant days of sunny April through the forest path he comes, comes, ever comes.

In the rainy gloom of July nights on the thundering chariot of clouds he comes, comes, ever comes.

In sorrow after sorrow it is his steps that press upon my heart, and it is the golden touch of his feet that makes my joy to shine.

Distant Time

I know not from what distant time thou art ever coming nearer to meet me. Thy sun and stars can never keep thee hidden from me for aye. In many a morning and eve thy footsteps have been heard and thy messenger has come within my heart and called me in secret. I know not only why today my life is all astir, and a feeling of tremulous joy is passing through my heart. It is as if the time were come to wind up my work, and I feel in the air a faint smell of thy sweet presence.

The Journey

The morning sea of silence broke into ripples of bird songs;
and the flowers were all merry by the roadside;
and the wealth of gold was scattered through
the rift of the clouds
while we busily went on our way and paid no heed.
We sang no glad songs nor played;

we went not to the village for barter;
we spoke not a word nor smiled;
we lingered not on the way.
We quickened our pace more and more as
the time sped by.
The sun rose to the mid sky and doves cooed in the shade.
Withered leaves danced and whirled in the hot air of noon.
The shepherd boy drowsed and dreamed in
the shadow of the banyan tree,
and I laid myself down by the water
and stretched my tired limbs on the grass.
My companions laughed at me in scorn;
they held their heads high and hurried on;
they never looked back nor rested;
they vanished in the distant blue haze.
They crossed many meadows and hills,
and passed through strange, far-away countries.
All honour to you, heroic host of the interminable path!
Mockery and reproach pricked me to rise,
but found no response in me.
I gave myself up for lost
in the depth of a glad humiliation
—in the shadow of a dim delight.
The repose of the sun-embroidered green gloom
slowly spread over my heart.
I forgot for what I had traveled,
and I surrendered my mind without struggle
to the maze of shadows and songs.
At last, when I woke from my slumber
and opened my eyes,
I saw thee standing by me, flooding my sleep
with thy smile.
How I had feared that the path was long and wearisome,
and the struggle to reach thee was hard!

Light

Light, my light, the world-filling light,
the eye-kissing light,

heart-sweetening light!
Ah, the light dances, my darling, at the centre of my life;
the light strikes, my darling, the chords of my love;
the sky opens, the wind runs wild, laughter
passes over the earth.
The butterflies spread their sails on the sea of light.
Lilies and jasmines surge up on the crest of
the waves of light.
The light is shattered into gold on every cloud, my darling,
and it scatters gems in profusion.
Mirth spreads from leaf to leaf, my darling,
and gladness without measure.
The heaven's river has drowned its banks
and the flood of joy is abroad.

Passing Breeze

Yes, I know, this is nothing but thy love,
O beloved of my heart—this golden light that
dances upon the leaves,
these idle clouds sailing across the sky,
this passing breeze leaving its coolness upon my forehead.
The morning light has flooded my eyes—
this is thy message to my heart.
Thy face is bent from above, thy eyes look
down on my eyes,
and my heart has touched thy feet.

Seashore

On the seashore of endless worlds children meet.
The infinite sky is motionless overhead
and the restless water is boisterous.
On the seashore of endless worlds
the children meet with shouts and dances.
They build their houses with sand
and they play with empty shells.
With withered leaves they weave their boats
and smilingly float them on the vast deep.
Children have their play on the seashore of worlds.

They know not how to swim, they know not
how to cast nets.
Pearl fishers dive for pearls, merchants sail in their ships,
while children gather pebbles and scatter them again.
They seek not for hidden treasures, they
know not how to cast nets.
The sea surges up with laughter
and pale gleams the smile of the sea beach.
Death-dealing waves sing meaningless
ballads to the children,
even like a mother while rocking her baby's cradle.
The sea plays with children,
and pale gleams the smile of the sea beach.
On the seashore of endless worlds children meet.
Tempest roams in the pathless sky,
ships get wrecked in the trackless water,
death is abroad and children play.
On the seashore of endless worlds is the
great meeting of children.

Colored Toys

When I bring to you colored toys, my child,
I understand why there is such a play of
colors on clouds, on water,
and why flowers are painted in tints
—when I give colored toys to you, my child.
When I sing to make you dance
I truly now why there is music in leaves,
and why waves send their chorus of voices to
the heart of the listening earth
—when I sing to make you dance.
When I bring sweet things to your greedy hands
I know why there is honey in the cup of the flowers
and why fruits are secretly filled with sweet juice
—when I bring sweet things to your greedy hands.
When I kiss your face to make you smile, my darling,
I surely understand what pleasure streams
from the sky in morning light,

and what delight that is that is which the summer
breeze brings to my body
—when I kiss you to make you smile.

Old and New

Thou hast made me known to friends whom I knew not. Thou hast given me seats in homes not my own. Thou hast brought the distant near and made a brother of the stranger. I am uneasy at heart when I have to leave my accustomed shelter; I forget that there abides the old in the new, and that there also thou abidest. Through birth and death, in this world or in others, wherever thou leadest me it is thou, the same, the one companion of my endless life who ever linkest my heart with bonds of joy to the unfamiliar. When one knows thee, then alien there is none, then no door is shut. Oh, grant me my prayer that I may never lose the bliss of the touch of the one in the play of many.

She

She who ever had remained in the depth of my being, in the twilight of gleams and of glimpses; she who never opened her veils in the morning light, will be my last gift to thee, my God, folded in my final song. Words have wooed yet failed to win her; persuasion has stretched to her its eager arms in vain. I have roamed from country to country keeping her in the core of my heart, and around her have risen and fallen the growth and decay of my life. Over my thoughts and actions, my slumbers and dreams, she reigned yet dwelled alone and apart. Many a man knocked at my door and asked for her and turned away in despair. There was none in the world who ever saw her face to face, and she remained in her loneliness waiting for thy recognition.

Stream of Life

The same stream of life that runs through my veins night and day runs through the world and dances in rhythmic measures. It is the same life that shoots in joy through the dust of the earth in numberless blades of grass and breaks into tumultuous waves of leaves and flowers. It is the same life that is rocked in the ocean-cradle of birth and of death, in ebb and in flow. I feel my limbs are made glorious by the touch of this world of life. And my pride is from the life-throb of ages dancing in my blood this moment.

Maya

That I should make much of myself and turn it on all sides, thus casting colored shadows on thy radiance —such is thy *Maya*. Thou settest a barrier in thine own being and then callest thy severed self in myriad notes. This thy self-separation has taken body in me. The poignant song is echoed through all the sky in many-coloued tears and smiles, alarms and hopes; waves rise up and sink again, dreams break and form. In me is thy own defeat of self. This screen that thou hast raised is painted with innumerable figures with the brush of the night and the day. Behind it thy seat is woven in wondrous mysteries of curves, casting away all barren lines of straightness. The great pageant of thee and me has overspread the sky. With the tune of thee and me all the air is vibrant, and all ages pass with the hiding and seeking of thee and me.

Innermost One

He it is, the innermost one, who awakens my being with his deep hidden touches. He it is who puts his enchantment upon these eyes and joyfully plays on the chords of my heart in varied cadence of pleasure and pain. He it is who weaves the web of this *maya* in evanescent hues of gold and silver, blue and green, and lets peep out through the folds his feet, at whose touch I forget myself. Days come and ages pass, and it is ever he who moves my heart in many a name, in many a guise, in many a rapture of joy and of sorrow.

Senses

Deliverance is not for me in renunciation. I feel the embrace of freedom in a thousand bonds of delight. Thou ever pourest for me the fresh draught of thy wine of various colours and fragrance, filling this earthen vessel to the brim. My world will light its hundred different lamps with thy flame and place them before the altar of thy temple. No, I will never shut the doors of my senses. The delights of sight and hearing and touch will bear thy delight. Yes, all my illusions will burn into illumination of joy, and all my desires ripen into fruits of love.

Face to Face

Day after day, O lord of my life, shall I stand before thee face to face. With folded hands, O lord of all worlds, shall I stand before thee face to face. Under thy great sky in solitude and silence, with humble heart shall I stand before thee face to face. In this laborious world of thine, tumultuous with toil and with struggle, among hurrying crowds shall I stand before thee face to face. And when my work shall be done in this world, O King of kings, alone and speechless shall I stand before thee face to face.

Lost Star

When the creation was new and all the stars shone in their first splendor, the gods held their assembly in the sky and sang 'Oh, the picture of perfection! the joy unalloyed!' But one cried of a sudden—'It seems that somewhere there is a break in the chain of light and one of the stars has been lost.' The golden string of their harp snapped, their song stopped, and they cried in dismay —'Yes, that lost star was the best, she was the glory of all heavens!' From that day the search is unceasing for her, and the cry goes on from one to the other that in her the world has lost its one joy! Only in the deepest silence of night the stars smile and whisper among themselves —'Vain is this seeking! unbroken perfection is over all!'

Let Me Not Forget

If it is not my portion to meet thee in this life then let me ever feel that I have missed thy sight —let me not forget for a moment, let me carry the pangs of this sorrow in my dreams and in my wakeful hours. As my days pass in the crowded market of this world and my hands grow full with the daily profits, let me ever feel that I have gained nothing —let me not forget for a moment, let me carry the pangs of this sorrow in my dreams and in my wakeful hours. When I sit by the roadside, tired and panting, when I spread my bed low in the dust, let me ever feel that the long journey is still before me — let me not forget a moment, let me carry the pangs of this sorrow in my dreams and in my wakeful hours.

When my rooms have been decked out and the flutes sound and the laughter there is loud, let me ever feel that I have not invited thee to my house —let me not forget for a moment, let me carry the pangs of this sorrow in my dreams and in my wakeful hours.

Roaming Cloud

I am like a remnant of a cloud of autumn uselessly roaming in the sky, O my sun ever-glorious! Thy touch has not yet melted my vapor, making me one with thy light, and thus I count months and years separated from thee. If this be thy wish and if this be thy play, then take this fleeting emptiness of mine, -paint it with colors, gild it with gold, float it on the wanton wind and spread it in varied wonders. And again when it shall be thy wish to end this play at night, I shall melt and vanish away in the dark, or it may be in a smile of the white morning, in a coolness of purity transparent.

Lost Time

On many an idle day have I grieved over lost time. But it is never lost, my lord. Thou hast taken every moment of my life in thine own hands. Hidden in the heart of things thou art nourishing seeds into sprouts, buds into blossoms, and ripening flowers into fruitfulness. I was tired and sleeping on my idle bed and imagined all work had ceased. In the morning I woke up and found my garden full with wonders of flowers.

Endless Time

Time is endless in thy hands, my lord. There is none to count thy minutes. Days and nights pass and ages bloom and fade like flowers. Thou knowest how to wait. Thy centuries follow each other perfecting a small wild flower.

We have no time to lose, and having no time we must scramble for a chance. We are too poor to be late. And thus it is that time goes by while I give it to every querulous man who claims it, and thine altar is empty of all offerings to the last. At the end of the day I hasten in fear lest thy gate be shut; but I find that yet there is time.

Chain of Pearls

Mother, I shall weave a chain of pearls for thy neck with my tears of sorrow. The stars have wrought their anklets of light to deck thy feet, but mine will hang upon thy breast. Wealth and fame come from thee and it is for thee to give or to withhold them. But this my sorrow is absolutely mine own, and when I bring it to thee as my offering thou rewardest me with thy grace.

Brink of Eternity

In desperate hope I go and search for her in all the corners of my room; I find her not. My house is small and what once has gone from it can never be regained. But infinite is thy mansion, my lord, and seeking her I have to come to thy door. I stand under the golden canopy of thine evening sky and I lift my eager eyes to thy face. I have come to the brink of eternity from which nothing can vanish —no hope, no happiness, no vision of a face seen through tears. Oh, dip my emptied life into that ocean, plunge it into the deepest fullness. Let me for once feel that lost sweet touch in the allness of the universe.

Untimely Leave

No more noisy, loud words from me—such is my master's will. Henceforth I deal in whispers. The speech of my heart will be carried on in murmurings of a song. Men hasten to the King's market. All the buyers and sellers are there. But I have my untimely leave in the middle of the day, in the thick of work. Let then the flowers come out in my garden, though it is not their time; and let the midday bees strike up their lazy hum. Full many an hour have I spent in the strife of the good and the evil, but now it is the pleasure of my playmate of the empty days to draw my heart on to him; and I know not why is this sudden call to what useless inconsequence!

Death

O thou the last fulfilment of life,
Death, my death, come and whisper to me!
Day after day I have kept watch for thee;
for thee have I borne the joys and pangs of life.
All that I am, that I have, that I hope and all my love
have ever flowed towards thee in depth of secrecy.
One final glance from thine eyes
and my life will be ever thine own.
The flowers have been woven
and the garland is ready for the bridegroom.
After the wedding the bride shall leave her home
and meet her lord alone in the solitude of night.

Last Curtain

I know that the day will come
when my sight of this earth shall be lost,
and life will take its leave in silence,
drawing the last curtain over my eyes.
Yet stars will watch at night,
and morning rise as before,
and hours heave like sea waves casting up pleasures and pains.
When I think of this end of my moments,
the barrier of the moments breaks
and I see by the light of death
thy world with its careless treasures.
Rare is its lowliest seat,
rare is its meanest of lives.
Things that I longed for in vain
and things that I got —let them pass.
Let me but truly possess
the things that I ever spurned
and overlooked.

Farewell

I have got my leave. Bid me farewell, my brothers!
I bow to you all and take my departure.
Here I give back the keys of my door
—and I give up all claims to my house.
I only ask for last kind words from you.
We were neighbors for long,
but I received more than I could give.
Now the day has dawned
and the lamp that lit my dark corner is out.
A summons has come and I am ready for my journey.

Threshold

I was not aware of the moment when I first crossed the threshold of this life. What was the power that made me open out into this vast mystery like a bud in the forest at midnight! When in the morning I looked upon the light I felt in a moment that I was no stranger in this world, that the inscrutable without name and form had taken me in its arms in the form of my own mother. Even so, in death the same unknown will appear as ever known to me. And because I love this life, I know I shall love death as well. The child cries out when from the right breast the mother takes it away, in the very next moment to find in the left one its consolation.

Parting Words

When I go from hence
let this be my parting word,
that what I have seen is unsurpassable.
I have tasted of the hidden honey of this lotus
that expands on the ocean of light,
and thus am I blessed
—let this be my parting word.
In this playhouse of infinite forms
I have had my play
and here have I caught sight of him that is formless.
My whole body and my limbs
have thrilled with his touch who is beyond touch;

and if the end comes here, let it come
—let this be my parting word.

Still Heart

When I give up the helm
I know that the time has come for thee to take it.
What there is to do will be instantly done.
Vain is this struggle.
Then take away your hands
and silently put up with your defeat, my heart,
and think it your good fortune to sit perfectly still
where you are placed.
These my lamps are blown out at every little puff of wind,
and trying to light them I forget all else again and again.
But I shall be wise this time and wait in the dark,
spreading my mat on the floor;
and whenever it is thy pleasure, my lord,
come silently and take thy seat here.

Ocean of Forms

I dive down into the depth of the ocean of forms, hoping to gain the perfect pearl of the formless. No more sailing from harbor to harbor with this my weather-beaten boat. The days are long passed when my sport was to be tossed on waves. And now I am eager to die into the deathless. Into the audience hall by the fathomless abyss where swells up the music of toneless strings I shall take this harp of my life. I shall tune it to the notes of forever, and when it has sobbed out its last utterance, lay down my silent harp at the feet of the silent.

Sit Smiling

I boasted among men that I had known you.
They see your pictures in all works of mine.
They come and ask me, 'Who is he?'
I know not how to answer them. I say, 'Indeed, I cannot tell.' They blame me and they go away in scorn. And you sit there smiling.
I put my tales of you into lasting songs.

The secret gushes out from my heart.
They come and ask me, 'Tell me all your meanings.'
I know not how to answer them.
I say, 'Ah, who knows what they mean!'
They smile and go away in utter scorn.
And you sit there smiling.

Salutation

In one salutation to thee, my God,

let all my senses spread out and touch this world at thy feet.

Like a rain-cloud of July hung low with its burden of unshed showers

let all my mind bend down at thy door in one salutation to thee.

Let all my songs gather together their diverse strains into a single current and flow to a sea of silence in one salutation to thee.

Like a flock of homesick cranes flying night and day back to their mountain nests let all my life take its voyage to its eternal home in one salutation to thee.

Chapter 7

Another Text by Rabindranath Tagore

My Heart like a Peacock on a Rainy Day.
by Rabindranath Tagore
My Heart Like a Peacock on a Rainy Day
O who is she on the king's tower
That has loosened the braid
on her dark hair,
has drawn over her breasts the blue veil?
She wildly starts and runs in the
sudden flashes of lighting
and lets the dark hair dance on her bosom.
Ah my heart dances like a peacock,
the rain patters on the new leaves of summer,
the tremor of the crickets' chirp troubles
the shade of the tree,
the river overflows its bank
washing the village meadows.
My heart dances.
The dumb earth looks into my face
and spreads her arms about me.
At nigh the fingers of the stars touch my dreams.
They know my former name.
Their whispers remind me of the music of a long
silent lullaby. They bring to my mind the smile of a
face seen in the gleam of the first daybreak.
There is love in each speck of earth
and joy in the spread of the sky.

I care not if I become dust, for the dust is touched by his feet. I care not if I become a flower, for the flower he takes up h his hand.

He is in the sea, on the shore, he is with the ship that carries all.

Whatever I am I am blessed and blessed in this earth of dear dust.

I threw away my heart in the world;
you took it up.
I sought for joy and gathered sorrow, you
gave me sorrow and I found joy.
My heart was scattered in pieces, you picked
them up in your hand and strung them in
a thread of love.
You let me wander from door to door to
show me at last how near you are.
Your love plunged me into the
deep trouble.
When I raised my head I found I was
at your door.
My heart, like a peacock on a rainy
day, spreads its plumes tinged with
rapturous colours of thoughts,
and its ecstasy seeks some
vision in the sky,—with a
longing for one whom it
does not know.
My heart dances.
The clouds rumble from sky
to sky—the shower seeps
horizons, the doves shiver
in silence in their nests,
the frogs croak in the
flooded fields—and the
clouds rumble.

—Rabindranath Tagore (1861-1941)

Chapter 8

Study Questions

Q. Discuss Tagore's Gitanjali as a work in the Bhakti Tradition?

Or

Q. Analyze how Tagore's Gitanjali as a reminiscent of a great Indian tradition

"The soul of music slumbers in the shell
Till waked and kindled by the master's spell
And feeling hearts – touch them but rightly- pour
A thousand melodies unfelt before."

Rabindranath Tagore's "Gitanjali" or "Song Offerings" written and translated into English by the poet himself, earned him world-wide acclaim. He was awarded the Nobel Prize in 1913. This essay analyzes how his poems from "Gitanjali" are reminiscent of a great Indian tradition called the Bhakti tradition.

In the 7th century A.D., the Bhakti cult propagated worship accompanied by music and dance. The Bhakti poets believed in surrender to the Godhead and in praising the name of the Lord in order to attain 'Mukthi' or salvation. The Bhakti yoga had two aspects to it – The Nirguna Bhakti and the Saguna Bhakti.

In Nirguna Bhakti, God or the Supreme power was a formless energy or force that had to be deeply felt and realized. These poets spoke of everyday activities as a service to God. They believed in love, surrender and in a universal religion.

The Saguna Bhakti tradition believed in a God who had a human form and personality endowed with supernatural qualities. These poets worshipped Vishnu or Siva as a God with a concrete form, abode and identity. They sang of pilgrim centres or temples where their God resided and stressed on total surrender of body, mind and soul to this Supreme Personality of Godhead.

"Gitanjali", written in 1912 is a string of devotional poems. Love is a major theme that connects all the verses in "Gitanjali" The God in "Gitanjali" has no name or abode and cannot be identified with any specific Indian God. He has His own form and personality. He is referred to as "You", "Thou" or "Thee" At times He is shown as a loving father who cares for His children and at times as a Lover who is waiting for reciprocation from His own creation.

The title "Gitanjali" or "Song Offerings" is in itself reminiscent of the Bhakti tradition. Bhakti poets such as Chaitanya, Mirabai and Aandal believed in worshipping God through music and dance highlighting performative nature of art in cultures with an oral tradition such as the ancient Tamil culture.

Music becomes an expression of infinite fountains of creativity that springs forth from the enlightened soul. Such music allows the devotee to string choice phrases together and sing the glory of God.

"This little flute of a reed thou hast carried over hills and dales, and hast breathed through it melodies eternally new" Gitanjali, I

Man becomes a mere instrument of carrying God's Love to the earth. The very music that the Bhakti poet renders is a gift from God, a divine expression that cannot be realized without the Grace of God.

"When thou commandest me to sing it seems that my heart would break with pride"

Gitanjali, II

The poet is "Drunk with the joy of singing" since he knows that he comes before God only as a singer. "All that is harsh and dissonant", in the poet's "life melts into one sweet harmony". The poet aspires to touch the unreachable feet of God with the "edge of the far-spreading wing of...song". The whole of life is seen as music made by God. "The light of thy music illumines the world. The life breath of thy music runs from sky to sky" says the poet.

In a similar tone Aandal says,

"Worldlings, listen to what we will do,
How observe these sacred days.
We will sing at the feet of that Supreme One."
Tiruppaavai I,2

He Bhakti poets had processions inviting one and all to sing the praise of the Lord. Amid clanging cymbals and drums, they sung the glory of God in Bhajans, simple and straightforward with cries of ecstasy which did not follow the strict rules of 'raag' or 'taal'.

"My song has put off her adornments...they would come between thee and me; their jingling would drown thy whispers...My poet's vanity dies in shame before thy sight."
Gitanjali, VII

Kabir condemns external telling of rosary beads and chanting of Rama's name. A true devotee does not make shows of his piety.

"Ram! Ram! they yell
till there's a callus on their tongue
They don't drink clean water
but yearn to dig a well."
[Ramaini, 33]

Tagore says,

"The child who is decked with prince's robes and has jewelled chains round his neck loses all pleasure in his play."
Gitanjali, VIII

Tagore's God loves simple expressions of devotion than extravagant displays of religious fervour.

"Here is thy footstool...where live the poorest and lowliest and lost..." Gitanjali, X

In Bhakthi poetry, the poet often demeans himself, while praising God.

Mahadevi Akka says,

"My body is dirt, my spirit is space: which shall I grab, O lord?"

Speaking of Siva, 12

Aandal says, "What a worm-eaten wood apple I am
Ague-stricken and sucked dry by his love!"
Nachiyar Tirumozhi, VIII

Tagore's devotion, however, goes one step further and believes that God's love is incomplete without reciprocation from man. Man becomes the receiver of God's love in its entirety.

A similar vein is to be found in Mahadevi Akka
" Dear girl go tell Him
bring Him back to His senses...
My lord white as jasmine
is angry
that we are two."
Speaking of Siva, 321

Influenced by Buddhism and its little expressions of local folk religions such as the religion of the Bauls, Tagore derives several of his images from Baul folk songs. The Bauls were mendicants. Their simple songs, set to a beautiful tune, sung with a one-stringed violin seemed to Tagore the greatest expression of Love for God. God, for the Bauls, was 'Love' in its supreme form. The Bauls considered the transient human body as a temple of God. Poems by Mahadevi Akka and Aandal capture the anguish in separation from God. Such pain the devotee goes through in pining for the Lord has been a major theme in Bhakti poetry.

"I cannot understand...
...my torture by south wind and moon
..I love him who straddled the world
And he leaves me in the lurch"
[Nachiyar Tirumozhi, V]

"Four parts of the day
I grieve for you.
Four parts of night
I'm mad for you.
I lie lost
sick for you, night and day,
O lord white as jasmine."
[Speaking of Siva, 79]

A devotee runs to the ends of the earth in search of God. At last, he rests to take a breath, weary with futility. At that moment of silence, God's Love springs upon him and takes him unawares. He realizes that God resides inside his very own soul.

"The traveller has to knock at every alien door to come to his own, and one has to wander through all the outer worlds to reach the innermost shrine at the end"

[Gitanjali, XII]

Mahadevi Akka says

"Not one, not two, not three or four,
but through eighty-four hundred thousand vaginas
have I come
through unlikely worlds.."

The ultimate realization that God is within oneself is also found in other Bhakti works. In one of Kabir's poems he says,

"Kabir says, clarity comes
when the musician lives
in your heart"

"Like
treasure hidden in the ground
taste in the fruit
gold in the rock
oil in the seed
the Absolute is hidden away
in the heart"

[Speaking of Siva, 2]

Tagore has captured this feeling in a couplet.

"The question and the cry `Oh, where?' melt into tears of a thousand streams and deluge the world with the flood of the assurance `I am!'" [Gitanjali, XII]

Separation from the loved one, waiting, searching, mourning and lamenting over the absence of the Supreme Lover are all common sentiments in the Bhakti tradition. The search is painful and the destination, elusive.

"When I awaken and hurry in search of my goal...cruelly thou hidest thyself before me"

[Gitanjali, XIV]

"Only there is agony of wishing in my heart...I live in the hope of meeting with him; but this meeting is not yet..." [Gitanjali, XIII]

Tagore expresses his ideas on the Vaishnava religion. He says it is similar to that of the Bauls while romanticizing the notion of God.

"God's love finding its finality in man's love... A

According to it, the lover, the man, is the complement of the Lover, God, in the internal love drama of existence"

[Tagore "An Indian Folk Religion"]

"O Mother, don't grieve. This my disease
No one can understand.
He whose hue is like the sea's
Can cure it with a touch."

[Nachiyar Tirumozhi, XII]

In his play, "Natir Puja", Tagore speaks of the simple and rebellious devotion of a dancer girl who dares defy the orders of King Ajatasatru to light lamps in a temple, the entry to which is forbidden to people of her clan. The punishment for her rebellion is death. The persecution that Mirabai, Mahadevi Akka and Aandal faced for their devotion is known to all. It must also be noted that Mahadevi Akka stripped herself naked and walked about covered only in her tresses. Her explanation for such a rebellion is like this:

"...can you peel
the Nothing, the Nakedness
that covers and veils?
To the shameless girl
wearing the White Jasmine Lord's
light of the morning,
you fool,
where's the need for cover and jewel?"

[Speaking of Siva, 124]

"Those who came to call me in vain have gone back in anger. I am only waiting for love to give myself up at last into his hands" [Gitanjali, XVII]

The sonority, the theme of surrender, love for the Lord, praise for the Lord, anguish in separation from the Lord and the final realization of God within oneself, are all features of Bhakti poetry.

"Like the colour in gold,
you were in me...
the paradox of your being
in me
without showing a limb"
[Speaking of Siva, 50]

Gitanjali is a masterpiece of devotion...

"In the pulsing life of dance,
To thee I raise
In wordless praise
My eager body's rhythmed cry –
This new birth's eloquence
In music and in gesture shines
My worship, Lord"
[Tagore, "Natir Puja"]

Q. Critically comment on Tagore's Gitanjali'

Or

Q. How can you say that the lines of Gitanjali are valid even today

Rabindra Nath Tagore (1861 - 1941), the celebrated poet, story writer and dramatist was awarded the Nobel Prize in Literature in 1913 (in the words of the Nobel Prize Committee) "because of his profoundly sensitive, fresh and beautiful verse, by which, with consummate skill, he has made his poetic thought, expressed in his own English words, a part of the literature of the West". His most famous poem 'Gitanjali' was originally written in Bengali language. Tagore was born in Bengal in 1861. He writings tasted initial success as a writer in his native Bengal. 'Gitanjali' ('song offerings'), is a collection of 103 poems. Originally written in Bengali, they were translated in English by Tagore himself. The characteristic feature of the collection is that the Introduction to Gitanjali was written by W.B.Yeats. Tagore had translated these songs from Bengali into English before his visit to England in 1912. His poems were well received in England.

'Gitanjali' begins with: "Thou hast made me endless, such

is thy pleasure. This frail vessel thou emptiest again and again, and fillest it ever with fresh life."

In one of the songs 'Where mind is without fear' Tagore has dreamed of a utopian land, a land of his dreams, a perfect place to live in.

"Where the mind is without fear and the head is held high;

Where knowledge is free;

Where the world has not been broken up into fragments by narrow domestic walls;

Where words come out from the depth of truth;

Where tireless striving stretches its arms towards perfection;

Where the clear stream of reason has not lost its way into the dreary desert sand of dead habit;

Where the mind is led forward by thee into ever-widening thought and action—

Into that heaven of freedom, my Father, let my country awake."

These are the vices present around us even today. The lines are as valid today as they might have been then. If we sketch a place in our minds according to the lines of this song, it would be like a heaven on this earth. May his dreams and wishes be fulfilled! This world would be a much better place to live in with only a fraction of those things coming true. Let's pledge to add a bit towards it on our part. Remember every drop counts!

Chapter 9

Criticism

Ryan D. Poquette

Poquette has a bachelor's degree in English and specializes in writing about literature. In the following essay, Poquette discusses the structure that Tagore uses in his poem.

When authors write prose poems, they do not need to pay as much attention to structure as when they write verse poetry. Blocks of prose can be as long or as short as the author wants, since the poetic elements like imagery and symbolism are what help to elevate the prose to prose poetry. However, when Tagore translated "60" into a prose poem from its Bengali-verse source, he paid close attention to the structure. Perhaps this is one reason why those who have commented on the poem like it so much. At first glance, the poem does not appear to be any different than many of Tagore's other nature poems. In her essay "Tagore's Lyric Poems," Mary M. Lago observes that "Nature is the touchstone, again and again, and it is a rare poem by Tagore that does not reflect in some way the skies, rivers, and landscape of Bengal.

" From the reviews of the few critics who have commented on "60," it seems that the poem is more than just one of Tagore's many reflections on nature. In his essay on Tagore for *Rabindranath Tagore: American Interpretations*, Melvin D. Palmer notes: "Only rarely do I find lines in Tagore that satisfy my hunger. One such is this, from *Gitanjali*, 60: 'On the seashore of endless worlds is the great meeting of children.'" Likewise, in his book *Passage to America: The Reception of Rabindranath Tagore in the United States, 1912 – 1941*, Sujit

Mukherjee comments on "60," which was also included in Tagore's later collection, *The Crescent Moon*: "One outstanding piece from *Gitanjali* included here under the title 'On the Seashore' is this volume's sole distinction." Finally, Yeats singled out this poem to conclude his laudatory introduction to *Gitanjali*.

By examining the structure of the poem, one can see why this poem has received almost universal praise. First, in broad terms, the poem is perfectly symmetrical in its thematic structure. The centre line of the third paragraph — the exact centre of the poem, in fact — anchors the poem in place. This sentence reads: "Pearl fishers dive for pearls, merchants sail in their ships, while children gather pebbles and scatter them again." This sentence stands on its own in the poem. No other sentence mentions the pearl fishers or merchants. However, every other sentence in the poem has a complementary sentence within its respective paragraph.

Continuing the example of the third paragraph, the paragraph starts with the following sentence: "They know not how to swim, they know not how to cast nets." Compare this with the last sentence of the third paragraph: "They seek not for hidden treasures, they know not how to cast nets." The first half of each unit mimics the style of the other, while the second half of each phrase is identical: "they know not how to cast nets." Moving from the centre of the poem outward to paragraphs two and four, one can see that these two paragraphs are also symmetrical.

Once again, the first and third sentences of each paragraph mirror each other in some way. In the second paragraph, the idea of playing on the sand is repeated in both the first and third sentence. In the fourth paragraph, the phrase "pale gleams the smile of the sea beach" is repeated in the first and third sentences. So is the motion of the sea. In the first sentence, the "sea surges." In the third sentence, the "sea plays." This symmetrical pattern continues in paragraphs one and five.

The symmetry is also apparent between corresponding paragraphs, not just sentences. In other words, while the first and third sentences of the first paragraph mirror each other, the first paragraph also mirrors its symmetrical partner, the fifth paragraph. When one looks at the poem as a whole, the symmetry of the paragraphs is as follows. Paragraphs one and five both feature the children meeting under a calm and violent sky. Paragraphs two and four feature, respectively, the children playing and the sea playing. And the lone middle paragraph describes the children's ignorance of adult, worldly ways. This pattern helps to emphasize the change in tone from calm to threatening.

If this were the only structural consistency, Tagore's poem would be considered neat and organized. However, Tagore takes it one step further. In addition to following a theme pattern in his sentences and paragraphs, he also follows a length pattern. Within each paragraph, the syllable length of each sentence can be described as long, medium, or short. No two sentences within any paragraph match each other in length, so there is always one long, one medium, and one short sentence. When one uses these designations to label each paragraph, another pattern emerges. For example, in the first paragraph, the first sentence is: "On the seashore of endless worlds children meet." This sentence is eleven syllables long, as compared to the middle sentence, which is twenty-two syllables long, and the last sentence, which is seventeen syllables long. This pattern of short/long/medium is repeated in the third and fifth paragraphs, and reversed in the second and fourth paragraphs. While this careful analysis of sentence length may not seem necessary, it does underscore Tagore's inventive structuring. Poets generally do not engage in such strict exercises of structure unless they have a purpose.

In this case, Tagore is giving each paragraph an ebb and flow pattern that mimics the waves moving from the sea to the shore and back. This ebb-and-flow pattern also holds up if one adds up the total number of syllables in each paragraph. The first, third, and fifth paragraphs are all medium length, while the second paragraph is short and the fourth paragraph is long. This structure gives the poem stability, which contrasts nicely with the instability discussed within the poem. In commenting on the "organic structure" of the poem,

Mukherjee observes that the whole is "controlled by contrasts that evolve out of the central opposition between the helpless children and the mighty sea." It is as if Tagore wishes to give his readers unstable and dangerous imagery, like the restless sea, but at the same time he wants to reassure them that it is okay. As Mukherjee notes, the idea of playing, as evidenced in the joyous meeting of children, is set up as a powerful ideological weapon against the fear of death. According to Mukherjee, "In the power of play lies the eternal triumph of life, as long as 'on the seashore of endless worlds there is the great meeting of children.'"

Tagore's focus on stability may also point to the political situation in India at the time. Although India was controlled by the British and torn by conflict, Tagore had high hopes that India would someday be independent and stable. He also hoped that he and other Indians would be able to reconcile the conflicting Eastern and Western ideals of his time. In his book *Rabindranath Tagore: His Mind and Art,* B. C. Chakravorty discusses one of Tagore's Bengali poems, which may or may not be the source of the English "60." Since Tagore radically changed his Bengali versions when converting them into the English *Gitanjali,* scholars do not usually know which Bengali poems correspond to the English poems.

However, most critics agree that Tagore retained the essence of the Bengali version in each English translation, and the seashore location of this Bengali poem sounds similar to the location in "60." Thus, Chakravorty comments about the Bengali poem: "Tagore conceives India as the meeting ground of different nations of the world." Everybody has "joined together on the seashore of humanity — that is India. From time immemorial India has cherished the ideal of unity." Whether or not this poem is talking about the same seashore, Chakravorty's comments are relevant to "60," since they indicate that Tagore's forced stability of the structure might signify his desire for political and cultural unity.

Symbolism in Tagore's Play, The Post Office

Symbols of Past, Present and Future India
By Alexander Preston,

While using symbolism to express controversial political views was not an invention of Tagore, his play, The Post Office, uses it effectively. Voltaire uses similar literary devices in his work, Candide, to express his views on optimism and to critique European governments. Tagore designed The Post Office to be deceptively simple. He keeps the character list short, and uses common language style. The main character is a small boy by the name of Amal.

The boy has an intense curiosity of the outside world, and yearns for the type of knowledge that can't be learned from a book. Another character is the Doctor, he is the man who diagnoses Amal, and will not let him leave the house because he is sick. On the other end of the spectrum you have Madhav, Amal's guardian. He is a man that believes in learning from Books, and feels more comfortable in home that outside.

The Dairyman is another character, he is a lowly curd peddler, not learned but experienced. The Watchman is a loyal servant to the king; he is knowledgeable of the government and King's systems. Along with this character is the Headman; he is an Indian who is placed in power by the king but not popular with the local population. Sudha is a girl, she gathers flowers, she is naïve and happy to do the work of her parents. Finally there is a group of boys, they encourage Amal to defy the doctor and leave the house. The understanding of Tagore's usage of symbolism in this play is central to understanding his ideology. Tagore was an Indian under British colonial rule. While Brittan had lost many of its colonies it still held onto India. Many Indians wanted to emancipate themselves from British rule and regain their sovereignty. However many Indians benefited from British rule and were content with the status quo. Throughout the play Tagore's symbols help explain the current state of India, and help to produce strong imagery of the past, present and future of the country.

Rabindranath Tagore as Reformer.

By Alex Ninian

Rabindranath Tagore: A Biography. Uma Das Gupta.

Oxford University Press. [pounds sterling]10.99. xii + 105 pages. ISBN 0-19-566980-0.

From this distance in time the eighty years of Rabindranath Tagore's life (1861-1941) are principally known for his work as a polymathic arts figure. He was not only a writer of novels, essays, and articles, a philosopher, a world-renowned poet and Nobel Prize winner. He also wrote songs and sang them; he wrote plays and acted in them; he wrote dance-dramas and danced in them. But, as they say, every schoolboy knows that.

What Uma Das Gupta has done here is quite deliberately to by-pass most of this and to bring out some lesser known and unsung parts of Tagore's life and work, and to delineate the forces that shaped his thinking and his work. The subjects examined here are his activities as an educator and rural reformer. His letters are evidence of how he longed only to be a poet, but they also reveal how he could not stay away from doing something practical and constructive for his country. Mr Gupta has chosen to write about these because, in his own words 'those aspects of his life are relatively unknown. We all know him as a poet but do not think of him as a man of action'.

Mainly, the focus is on Tagore's practical actions in creating Visva-Bharati, an educational institution—even a university—in rural Bengal, and on his work to improve the economic, social, physical and cultural well-being of villagers in the countryside. A secondary theme of the book is to identify and elaborate on the issues and beliefs that concerned Tagore all his life as a poet and a writer. This follows his privileged upbringing in British India and his travels all over the world to illustrate how his convictions were developed about Indian history, nationalism and internationalism, racial humiliation, self-esteem and humanism.

Without actually saying so in so many words, the author brings out the interplay of nature and nurture—of inherent character and the effect of environment. Tagore was a deeply independent and unorthodox personality who found a way of expressing this through the fashions and orthodoxies of his environment. He rejected imperialism in advance of many of his fellows, and then rejected nationalism when that became the political mantra. He adored his native land, its people, its religion and its history but was appalled by its illiteracy and ignorance. This interplay brought him to reject politics as a way of doing things and led to his conviction that, in his own words 'all human problems find their fundamental solution in education'. His version of religion was humanism, the 'religion of man'.

The culmination of this was the Santiniketan school whose aim was to be the model for the improvement of the people through not only literacy but humanist philosophy, singing, dancing and the arts. This, in turn, developed in a practical way to the institute of rural reconstruction which worked with village people to develop roads, schools, reservoirs, sanitation and to improve agriculture by the use of fertilizers and mechanisation. The appendix of selected letters by Rabindranath Tagore will be of special interest to students as well as to readers with a deep interest in his life. These include correspondence with Nehru as well as the actual letter to Lord Chelmsford in 1919 renouncing the knighthood he had accepted from George V. The renunciation was in protest at the severity of British measures to quell disturbances in Punjab.

Mr Gupta has set out the limits of his study and, within these, has done what he set out to do—to highlight the little known actions of Tagore and the background to them

The Indian novel in England

The 'deep association' that Rabindranath Tagore welcomed between India and the West as far back as 1916 has by today gone far beyond anything the imperial encounter could have anticipated.

In a world routinely described in terms of the prefix 'post' (as in post-modern, post-colonial etc.) cultures are seen in the images of pyramids and cities as melting pots full of sociological chop suey. Given those new circumstances the very title of Salman Rushdie's East, West (published last year) catches the mongrel spirit of our times definitively; with the matter-of-factness of the Rudyard Kipling line, 'East is East and West is West and never the twain shall meet', which, in another era, indicated the exact opposite.

What puts such a psychological distance between 'East is East etc.' and East, West is, of course, historical time. The presence of the British Raj in India as described in Kipling's Kim, Plain Tales from the Hills, Wee Willie Winkie etc. and even E. M. Forster's A Passage to India brought into being a literary terrain called Anglo-India. The point of view from that place was implicitly that of the colonial expatriate. In that world it was not pukka to mix overtly with the locals.

Since Indian independence in 1947 and the migrations from the subcontinent into Britain which followed, new possibilities - socially, culturally, artistically - had to emerge. For reasons such as these English literature was becoming a literature in English. When Rushdie's Midnight's Children won the Booker Prize in Britain in 1982 this seemed confirmed, at least in the eyes of a certain reading public. As a former advertising copywriter and ever keen to coin a phrase, Rushdie heralded the discovery of a new fictional land: Indo-Anglia.

In an influential article in The Times that year he continued to clear the ground, escalating the tone with playful effrontery: English, no longer an English language, now grows from many roots; and those whom it once colonized are carving out large territories for themselves. The Empire is striking back.

The battle over English is not new, and neither is the struggle to belong within the canon of English studies. The growth of literary criticism this century can be seen as a kind of postal sorting of great from good writing. F. R. Leavis' The Great Tradition which appeared in 1948, among other things helped to fasten Jane Austen, George Eliot, Henry James and Joseph Conrad onto an English readers' royal family tree. The first stirrings of activity in Indo-Anglia began, curiously enough, at around this time.

V. S. Naipaul, of Indian extraction but from Trinidad, arrived in Britain in 1950. Eight years later he claimed despondently that the Americans didn't want him because he was too British, and that the British public didn't want him because he was too foreign. 'It is an odd situation', he wrote, 'an Indian writer writing in English for an English audience about non-English characters who talk their own sort of English.'

What established Naipaul into what might be considered today a pantheon of world writers was the publication in 1961 of his novel, A House for Mr. Biswas. The central tension of a man caught between his desire for independence and the irresistible pull of the Hindu family structure - all within a post-colonial Trinidad setting - was unique in its local flavour; yet, like much great literature, universal in its portents.

Critics rushed to make hay out of Biswas and apportioned him a plethora of literary forbears; comparisons with characters out of Dickens, Dostoyevsky and even Beckett abounded. The forging of possible links between texts is for readers and scholars alike always interesting. All the more if they are from culturally if not linguistically different sources.

And yet, the text that reverberates most influentially at the heart of A House for Mr. Biswas is not from the Western tradition. It is, instead, the Ramayana, one of the two sacred Hindu texts, the Mahabharata being the other. According to R. K. Narayan, all imaginative writing in India has its origins in these books.

What was remarkable about Naipaul's novel at the time was its portrayal of an aspect of Indian life enacted outside India. It is one of the first modern novels to observe the conundrums of the post-colonial condition in the novel form. Central to this is an underlying tension between inescapable past and unyielding present, with the individual caught inexorably in the middle.

Biswas is by turns heroic and pathetic in trying to resist his in-laws who live at the heavily symbolic Hanuman House. The Ramayana - in which the monkey Hanuman is a major character - rescues and ruins him. During a re-enactment of King Lear's heath scene Biswas begins to chant with sudden piety, Rama Rama Sita Rama - Rama and Sita being the hero and heroine of the Ramayana.

The ritual chanting of this mantra, as recommended by

the ancient text itself, saves him and damns him too. Such a state of contradiction is a quintessential Indo-Anglian limbo. One which was to inform Naipaul's work to such a point that by the 1970s the novelist and travel writer, Paul Theroux, was commenting that '[he] is the first in his line, without a tradition or home'.

The most fervent political mantra on Indian lips this century was without question Quit India. As the events of 1947 (when independence was gained) and 1948 (when the last Viceroy, Lord Mountbatten, finally left) reflected, words themselves (not only chanted but also inscribed on every wall of every city, town and village) seemed to move the hand of fateful action. But in spite of India and Britain's 'unholy wedlock, deadlock and divorce', as Narayan has put it, the deep association has grown.

Even a sombre and domestic drama such as Anita Desai's Clear Light of Day, published in 1980, cannot shake off the anxiety of influence. Intertextuality, or the way outside works echo in the reading of another, is very active beneath the calm surface. From the works of Eliot, Tennyson, Lawrence and Swinburne to the Urdu poet, Iqbal, there are epigraphs, allusions and quotations. And yet, Desai's story is but a quiet family reminiscence of the summer of 1947 in India. At fiction's altar two histories and two literatures, Indian and English, become conjugated once more.

'Rushdie's Midnight's Children, published in 1981, has become a central text in many genres, including magical realism and what is known as Commonwealth literature. Like Gabriel Garcia Marquez' One Hundred Years of Solitude and Gunther Grass' The Tin Drum, it is a novel that seems to speak for an entire continent. As in Clear Light of Day, the subject of Midnight's Children is 1947. The style of observation, however, could not be more different. For a definitive account of the intertextual influences on the writing of that novel the clearest commentator is the writer himself. His collection of essays entitled Imaginary Homelands, published in 1991, is a superb reader's companion not only to this book but to the Indo-Anglian disposition in general.

Rushdie's assertion that a book is 'a kind of passport' is a poignant one. He has spent most of this decade in hiding because of the late Ayatollah Khomenei's fatwa issued against him for his novel The Satanic Verses, published in 1988, which accused him of blasphemy against Islam. Artistically, at least, he remains a free spirit. He admits to roaming from Ted Hughes's Crow poems to Sergei Eisenstein's The Film Sense to Eugene Ionesco's Rhinoceros, and perhaps more crucially to Laurence Sterne's Tristram Shandy for inspiration.

It is worth noting that these names are drawn not only from various countries but also from various genres of art. With the actual diaspora of peoples has come a timeless and boundary-less meeting of minds and fusion of ideas. Indeed, at one point in Midnight's Children the narrator, Saleem, complains helplessly about the 'polyglot frenzy in my head'.

By 1991 the borders of Indo-Anglia had been extended irrevocably into the cultural mainstream. So much so that Time magazine could run a major feature entitled 'Rushdie's Children'. Rushdie himself, having claimed ten years earlier, 'I think we are in a position to conquer English literature', was now being perceived as a patriarch in the house of fiction. By the time Midnight's Children was named 'Booker of Bookers' in 1993 Leavis's great English tradition had become, if popular prizes are any measure to go by, a multicoloured and multifarious spectrum.

In the days of empire, when a sahib's tour of service on the sub-continent was complete, retirement back to England (read: civilization) was de rigueur. To stay on was a rare thing and strongly disapproved of. Going 'jungli' or native, and adopting local customs was an unforgivable act in the imperial code of practice.

The irony, of course, is that one of the standards of English civilization, the English novel, has itself gone 'jungli'. It has become complicated with the new inflections of hitherto 'strange' voices. For Indo-Anglian writers since Rushdie's breakthrough, one of the prevalent concerns has been in locating a strong conception of selfhood in the post-modern pell-mell. Hybrid cultures can seem to fall between two stools.

Thus, forging a genuine sense of identity at the twain of granite-like myth and knee-jerk stereotyping has been in no small way the Asian man's burden.

By the late 1970s in Britain the most significant cultural encounter was between black and white, particularly in popular music. The idea of a 'two-tone' youth culture had a supposed universal appeal and yet the Asian element did not seem to play an active part in it. The British born, Hanif Khureishi, has observed this chasm well in his script for the 1986 film My Beautiful Launderette, and his novel The Buddha of Surburbia, published in 1990.

The central dilemma that affects his protagonists is whether to 'act coloured' and remain near to stereotype, or escape this by 'bleaching' one's roots. There is a constant play-off between the authentic and the phoney. Karim, the central character in The Buddha of Suburbia is, admittedly, 'an Englishman born and bred, almost... having emerged from two old histories'. His identity crisis reaches tragi-comical heights when he agrees to play Mowgli in a stage production of Kipling's The Jungle Book, or as he puts it, 'The Jungle Bunny Book'.

In response to the cheeky view that Britain's national dish is the chicken curry, comes Farrukh Dhondy's novel Bombay Duck, also published in 1990. It takes off on the ideas and idiosynchrosies of take-away culture. That Bombay duck, a favourite side-dish on the curry house menu is nothing like poultry and is, in fact, an oderous dried fish is just one hint that Bombay Duck is about things not being what they at first seem.

Stepping beyond the imaginary India of 1947, Dhondy skilfully takes swatches out of and swipes at modern day Britain; at the accents and attitudes, the races and relations. His satirical touch is a deft one. The social foibles and hypocrisies of Anglified Indians and Indianized Britons are engagingly critiqued without being morally judged. It provides a timely antidote to the kind of political correctness that reaches for its gun whenever race or sex is alluded to in anything but a positive way.

Bombay Duck is an insightful sign of the times in Indo-Anglia. It does not seek to answer its own questions; one of which is posed when a British stage version of the Ramayana is put on in India and it receives a hostile, even murderous reception. When an authentically 'Indian' version of it arrives in Britain, however, it is forced to shut down due to widespread lack of interest.

Between the extremes of an emotionally charged tradition and the prospect of an apathetic, mixed up here and now: that is still the limbo, even into the 1990s, in which the fantasy world of Indo-Anglia must continue to discover itself. Forster's famous farewell at the end of A Passage to India, when nature itself speaks to defer a real meeting between Indian and Englishman - 'No, not yet', and the sky said, 'No, not there' - has never sounded so distant.

configuration, like clouds floating in the sky. If these aimless reflections could somehow be recorded on pieces of canvas, we would find some similarity between these pictures and our rhymes. These rhymes are simply reflections of our ever-changing inner mind; they are like the fluid shadows of clouds on the clear waters of a lake. This is why I say that rhymes are born spontaneously.

Before examining some of these rhymes for illustration, I have several apologies to make to my readers. First, how am I, an aged, somber, and status-conscious man, to capture the soft, loving, and simple voices that are eternally associated with the telling of these rhymes? I fear that readers will have to contribute that tender essence from their own childhood memories. With what magic can I bring back the love, the tunes, the memories of softly lit evenings with which these rhymes are forever linked? I can only hope that at least some of that charm has been captured in the following lines. Second, it may impinge on these homely, simple, and unadorned womanly rhymes to place them in the company of tight, rigorous, and sophisticated essays, somewhat like presenting a simple, naive housewife as a witness in a court of law. But there is no other choice; courts must run according to their rules, and essays must be written according to theirs. The associated pain is unavoidable. Jamunabati Saraswati, tomorrow is her wedding, Jamuna will travel to her groom's through Kajitala. While picking kaji flowers, I found a garland, Tinkling bells on hands and feet, it's Sitaram's game. Dance dear Sitaram, bend your hips, I'll feed you a tapal full of rice. The throat got parched while eating the rice, There's no water here, go to Tripurni's ghat. Two fish swim near the banks of Tripurni, Guruthakur took one of them, someone else took the other, I marry his sister with oarflowers. The day wore on while we picked oarflowers, I marry his sister at high noon.

Even the most sympathetic critic will have to admit that there is absolutely no relationship between the respective thoughts in this rhyme. A series of pictures floats by, one after another. One thing is clear, though - there is no sense of discrimination. It is as if the guard at the gate of high poesy is enjoying a siesta in the sweet warmth of a fall afternoon, and truant thoughts, taking full advantage of the situation, are freely coming and going without so much as a word of introduction or excuse. Sometimes they even skip over the poor guard's outstretched legs or gently nudge his ears as they gambol carefree inside the magnificent edifice of the human imagination. If the guard suddenly wakes up, though, these thoughts will not know where to run.

Whoever Jamunabati Saraswati is, it is clear that tomorrow is the big day of her wedding. It may not have been necessary at this point to mention the route she has to take through Kajitala on the way to her groom's house, but then, it is not entirely irrelevant either. However, there is absolutely no indication of any preparation for the occasion, and no one seems the least interested in it. The land of rhyme is such a place. There things happen, or do not happen, with such ease that no one ever worries. Thus, although Miss Jamunabati is to be married the next day, no one pays much attention; indeed, no one even asks why the subject came up. As a city dweller I am not familiar with kaji flowers, but I am certain that the upcoming wedding has no relation to the picking of such flowers. Furthermore, I am at a total loss to explain why suddenly, in the midst of all this confusion, Sitaram starts dancing with tinkling bells on his hands and feet. The lure of rice may have done the trick, but again, the same rice distracts us from Sitaram's performance and takes us to the banks of the Tripurni. Although it is not surprising to find two fish swimming near the banks of this river, it is surprising that our determined composer intends to marry the sister of the completely unknown man who claims the second fish for himself. Moreover, he ignores all civilized norms for a proper wedding by deciding to conclude the auspicious ceremony with oarflowers, and I am certain that the time of the event was not chosen on the basis of any calendar, old or new.

So much for poetic content. If the plot had been ours to develop, we would most certainly have made Jamunabati the sister of the unknown man at the end of the story, and would have concluded the high-noon ceremony between her and our composer with the help of the oarflowers. Such a turn of events would surely have brought greater aesthetic pleasure to the reader.

The mind of the child, however, is for the most part free of such conscious rigor. The child is affected independently by his own imagination and by the outside world; one arrives after the other. The fetters of the conscious mind are distressing for children; they find it difficult to pursue anything along a well-defined path of cause and effect. Children build castles in their minds just as they build sand castles by the shore. Sand lacks the ability to stick together, so the castles are not solid. But it is precisely this quality that makes sand suitable for the creations of children. One can build a grand structure in minutes with fistfuls of sand, and if the architecture turns out not to be to one's liking one can easily correct the mistakes. The playful creator, when exhausted, can instantly level the structure with a kick and happily return home.

When one builds by design, however, one is forced to follow the rules of building. Children are incapable of adhering to such rules - they have only recently arrived from the carefree, cheerful, and impulsive land of the gods. Unlike us, they are not yet used to long periods of servility. The child, building castles in the sand and forming rhyming images in his mind, imitates in this mortal world the actions of our Creator. That is why our scriptures often equate the actions of the Creator with the play of a child both are products of carefree and joyous fancy.

The rhyme quoted above has no coherence, yet it does present images. The events at Kajitala, at Oarforest, and on the banks of Tripurni are as strange as those in a dream, but are just as real.

I ask the reader to bear with me when I claim that dreams are real. Many eminent philosophers have questioned the reality of the present world, but the same skeptics have been unable to doubt the reality of dreams. "There is no such thing as reality," they have said. So what is there? The answer is dreams. Thus you can see that though the actuality of this world can be denied with the help of sophisticated arguments, it is not so easy to deny the reality of dreams. Here I refer not only to daydreams or conscious flights of imagination; my point is equally valid for unconscious dreams during sleep. It is absolutely impossible for even the most committed skeptic to doubt his own dreams while he is dreaming them himself. People who continually doubt even the simplest of truths while awake willingly accept the reality of dreams while asleep. Thus a prime quality associated with truth - believability - is present to an unequaled extent in dreams.

The reader will realise from the above that the world of dreams is far more real to a fanciful and imaginative child than the real world is to an adult. That is why, while we adults sometimes reject truths as improbable, children easily accept the impossible as true.

The rain falls tip tap, the river gets flooded. Shivuthakur weds on such a day, Three maidens are given away. The first maiden cooks and cleans, The second one just feeds, The third one returns to her parents without eating anything.

When I hear this rhyme now I cannot but admire the wisdom of the second of Shivuthakur's three brides. But there was a time when I did not possess such shrewd powers of character analysis. These few lines were like the classic epic Meghaduta to me at that time. I could vividly see a majestic, heaving river rushing downstream on a dark and stormy day. I could also see a few small boats moored by the bank and the three new brides of our Shivuthakur busy preparing the evening meal. To tell you the truth, I was quite moved by the charming life of this man. Even my concerns for the temperamental third maiden and her brisk retreat to her parents' home could not mar the beauty of this image. An inexperienced young lad, I could not comprehend that in these lines the disastrous, heartrending end of Shivuthakur's married life was being portrayed. But, as I have already said, at that age I was busier fashioning images than analyzing human nature. Only now do I realise that the unfortunate Shivuthakur did not take his third bride's desertion in the same blissful spirit that I did.

Sometimes I wonder about this Shivuthakur. Perhaps someone of that name really existed. It is possible that a fragment of some forgotten history survives in these lines. Other rhymes may contain other fragments of the same man's life story.

Ganga on this side, Ganga on the other, A piece of land lies in between, Shiv Sadagar remains seated in the middle. He went to his in-laws' house, They gave him a seat to sit, Offered him a snack of shalirice chira [rice flakes]. It was not shalirice chira silly, It was only binnirice khoi [puffed rice], Along with some big delicious bananas and curd from Kagmari.

From the description I suspect that Shivuthakur and Shiv Sadagar are the same person. Both are quite conscientious in their marital duties and perhaps rather mindful of their eating habits. One also has to admire Shiv Sadagar's choice of a small island in the middle of the Ganga as the place to spend his newly wedded life.

The careful reader will notice that shalirice chira is mistakenly mentioned at first as a snack appropriate for Shiv Sadagar, but that the error is quickly rectified and binnirice khoi identified as the snack of choice, as if there can be no excuse for having misrepresented such an important incident. It must be admitted, though, that this substitution does not greatly improve the quality of the food, nor the in-law's reputation for hospitality. Perhaps our composer was more concerned with presenting the truth than with anything else. But that does not appear likely either! Could this be like a dream, with the shalirice chira having somehow changed itself into binnirice khoi between one glance and the next? Who can say that Shivuthakur did not similarly transform himself into Shiv Sadagar?

We are told that there are fragments of rock between Mars and Jupiter; some maintain that these are the broken bits of an entire planet. To me these children's rhymes are like similar fragments of some erstwhile existence. Many broken bits of ancient lives and memories are scattered amongst them, and no archeologist can ever put them back together again. Only our imagination can sometimes capture the essence of those distant, lost lives.

A child's mind, however, is not particularly interested in reconstructing such historical entities. The child lives in the present, and that is what is glorious and important to him. All he cares about are concrete pictures; he does not wish to blur them with emotional tears. Notice how a series of images floats across the following passage, like a flock of birds. Each and every picture is impressed upon the child's mind separately, but deeply.

The white pigeons strut their feathers While the ladies come to bathe in the river. Two carps swim near the surface, Brother had a pen which he threw at them. Two girls stepped into the water, Their bangles tinkle in the wind. Who had kept it? Must be my brother. Today's brother's bachelor's day, Tomorrow's his wedding. What route is he going to take? He'll travel through Bakultala. I found a garland while picking bakul flowers. Ramdhanuk's drum beats on As Sitanath continues reveling. Sitanath says, I want to eat some chalkarai [roasted beans] - Too much of it parched my throat. Wandered around here and there, came to the Chitpur field. The sands shimmer in the midday sun, The pretty face looks bloodshot in the heat.

None of the above pictures captures us for long, nor can we cling to them for long. The quick-flowing images of strutting white pigeons, approaching ladies, fish swimming near the bank, girls bathing on the other side, a brother's impending wedding, Sitanath's frolicking in time to Ramdhanuk's drum, a charming face crimson at midday on a lonely sandy field - all of these pictures have a dream-like quality. The distant imagery of two girls emerging from the water, the faint tinkling of their bangles audible from this shore, are as real as a dream, and like dreams they do not follow any planned design.

The reader must remember at this point that one cannot deliberately create a dream. The rhymes above may have been written effortlessly under the impulse of carefree fancy, but such a sense of the carefree cannot be consciously captured. We have conditioned ourselves to conscious and directed effort, and thus simple and natural things have become terribly difficult. A mood of anxious stress shadows all our efforts even when totally uncalled for. The moment such feelings make their presence felt, all carefree impulses and fancies congeal and lose their freedom to fly. That is why I maintain that those who are able to compose children's rhymes do it naturally, while those who have to make the least bit of effort find the task impossible. The simplest things are actually the hardest to accomplish - that is the prime quality of simplicity

The reader must have also noticed that our first rhyme has somehow managed to merge itself with this one. Rhymes, like dreams or passing clouds, continuously melt into one another, and no critic blames anyone of plagiarism or distortion of thoughts. These rhymes are like wisps of clouds in the vast expanse of our mind, and there is no way to delineate limits or boundaries between them. Rules or regulations are totally out of place here. Notice the next set of rhymes:

The Janti tree on the other side is full of fruit. I ate too much fruit, and now I feel ill at ease - My throat is parched, I am miserable, When do we go to the field of Haragauri? Haragauri's field is covered with ripe paddy. Bought some lime and pan [betel leaves], shared it with my sister-in-law, Reported to my brother when a pan got lost. Called my brother a few times, he was not at home, Called Subal a few times, Subal was at home. Today is Subal's bachelor's day, tomorrow is his wedding, We shall take him through Dignagar. The girls at Dignagar are busy washing themselves, Their thick black tresses drape them. They are busy drying their glistening hair, Their conch bangles are as white as the clouds. Their red takti [coral] necklaces are blood red, Striped saris drape their slim figures. Two big fish swim close to the bank, Guruthakur took one of them, the other was claimed by the parakeet, It's the parakeet's mom's wedding with a red handkerchief And fig leaves. The bride's name is Gouri, The groom is our Noka. The drum rolls on, their home is in Charakdanga.

Attempts to get a realistic picture from these fragments will lead us nowhere. In the rhyme on page 8, above, the frolicking boy Sitaram, thirsty from eating too much rice, brings us to the Tripurni's bank. A later rhyme describes how Sitanath ended up in the field of Chitpur in search of water, thirsty from munching on chalkarai. The rhyme immediately above depicts how a poor girl and her spiteful sister-in-law went to the field of Haragauri after injudiciously consuming some wild berries, and how the latter searches up and down the village for her brother to report his wife's momentary carelessness.

Such is the degree of connection between these three rhymes. The incidents in the individual rhymes are also rather weakly linked. And it is quite clear that most of the descriptions are products of fanciful imaginations. Fabrications are usually presented with an excess of explanation in an attempt to make them appear plausible, but there is no such effort here. The events described in the rhymes are neither true nor false - they are completely beyond any such distinctions. Notice the mention of Subal's wedding. Though not a particularly unlikely event, one does wonder why it is introduced at this point.

Called my brother a few times, he was not at home, Called Subal a few times, Subal was at home. Today is Subal's bachelor's day, tomorrow is his wedding.

As soon as the name Subal appears the rhyme takes

control, and Subal's wedding is settled in an instant. But this topic does not tarry long either: soon the long-haired maidens of Dignagar capture our attention. This is precisely what happens in a dream. Images jump from one to another on a chain of similar-sounding words or trivial thoughts. Images emerge for a fleeting moment, then dissolve only to reappear as something totally different in the next. No one expresses any concern about the probability of these events. They live for no more than an instant before dissolving into the next portrait. Just as a particular picture is nonexistent until the moment of its birth, so it removes itself, instantly and effortlessly, from the realm of possibility following the rhythms of word association. Thus even if Subal's impending wedding is not so improbable, readers would have to agree that the wedding of a parakeet's mother with the aid of a red handkerchief is totally out of the question in this world of ours. But rigorous reasoning like this is absolutely useless to those interested only in creating and visualizing word-pictures according to the natural cadence of language.

This is all the more so with children, whose imaginative powers are far more acute than those of adults. Earlier I referred to the divine quality of the child's impulsive creativity. We grown-ups can never create as easily as children. Think how difficult it would be for an adult to arouse feelings of love and nurture toward a doll of knotted rag and treat it like a human child. For us to imagine something as human we need to make it resemble the human form as closely as possible - our weak imaginations bridle at the minutest deviation from reality. Adults are completely controlled by the rules of the material world; we are unable to imagine things without the help of our visual impressions.

Children, however, are capable of letting their fancy take wing at the slightest hint from their eyes, their natural creativity making up for all shortcomings. That is why they can so easily love as human a mere piece of rag. It must be pointed out, too, that the appeal of these images is not limited to children. They move a hard-headed adult just as deeply; in fact, the descriptions are so crisp that they instantly bring visions to even the most skeptical of eyes. They are like pencil sketches in which a few strokes suggest an entire picture. Just as a matchstick can produce a flame in an instant, a single word can immediately evoke an image. Although not the work of a patient craftsman, a description like "Wandered around here and there, came to the Chitpur field; The sands shimmer in the midday sun" instantly transports us to a wide and fallow sandy field on a hot, dry summer afternoon. Similarly, "Striped saris drape their slim figures" is a quite accurate depiction of the way the folds of a flowing sari, like currents in a tiny whirlpool, adorn a charming figure. A variant says, "The striped sari flows around her," a not unattractive portrayal either. Another rhyme goes: Come sleep, O come sleep to the Bagdi village. Their boy sleeps, cuddling up with a fishnet.

The reader can instantly visualize the Bagdi child fast asleep in a corner, cuddled up with a fishnet. Again, note the following rhyme:

Come on boys, let us go fishing. A fish bone pricked my feet, So let's hop on a ride and count our coins as we go. The water near this bank is filled to the brim, The sand on this bank crumbles down, The pretty face is flushed in the midday sun.

Even if the reader dismisses the first three lines as inconsequential, it would be hard for him to deny the picturesque yet concise nature of the second three lines' description of a swollen river with crumbling sand banks.

There is another category of rhymes that manages in a few spare lines to portray an entire way of life. Sometimes the mention of an apparently trivial detail can evoke an image of the Bengali village that instantly touches our hearts. Such trivial details do not easily find their way into the high-flowing descriptions of stylish prose. And any attempt to put them there would transform them into something these homely rhymes are not. Look, for example, at the simple beauty of the following lines:

Dear brother, a city traveller, You earn a salary of three rupees. I place a tulsi [basil] garland on your neck, How fine a groom will you make. Dear brother, I fall on your feet, Bring home a wife, so that I can play with her.

The brother does not earn much, but to his younger sister it is a princely sum indeed. Citing his salary, she implores him to bring home a playmate for her. The girl also knows how to tease him into a promise, softening him up with references to his manly charm. I suspect that the brother readily obliged his sister despite the expense involved in granting her wish, and I am sure he did not do so simply to fulfill his brotherly obligations.

Get ready, rejoice, madar flowers, The groom is on his way, How far is he from here? Is he at Baghnapara? O dear sister, get on with your cooking, You, young maiden, go fetch some water. Weeds float in the water, Flowers bloom in there, They are white as shells. A dish of kale and crumbs.

The image of busy, curious village women keenly awaiting the arrival of a groom is accurately captured by this rhyme, and a Bengali village with its rustic wooden fences and muddy walkways along the ponds appears magically before our eyes. Almost every such rhyme gives us a glimpse of a way of life, reminding us of long-forgotten rustic tunes or leading us into the plain but charming households of Bengali villagers.

Sometimes the pictures drawn in these rhymes are quite fanciful, but I see no problem with that. Fantasy, in fact, may be the best thing. We in our lack of awareness need an unconventional approach. To children there is nothing outlandish, since in their world everything is possible. No child has run to the last limits of reality and come back empty-handed. In his logic, if one thing is possible then anything is possible. If one thing is not considered strange, then why should another thing be? A child says, "I accept the idea of a one-headed person without question since I see one in front of me. I also do not question the reality of a two-headed person because I can easily see such a being in my mind. A headless man is just as real to me because he is perfectly imaginable."

There is an interesting story in this context. A man said to his friends, "I saw a curious thing on my way here. A person got beheaded in a fight, but he still walked ten steps." His friends said, "What? He actually took ten steps?" There was a woman in the group, however, who said, "I don't find it strange that he took ten steps. What is strange is the fact that he managed to take the first step!" Likewise, the first act of creation is what is curious; that is the biggest miracle, not that other marvelous things follow. The child has yet to lose his fascination with this first marvel. With his first glimpse of the world he starts to wonder about everything around him - that is why he is quite willing to accept the reality of anything. Thus in the world of rhymes there is no conflict between the land of the real and the land of the unreal.

Come, dear Parakeet, Come in a sailboat. The carp took the boat, The beaver frolicked at the sight. Beaver, beaver look around, See my child's delight.

No child can claim to have seen at any time in his life a parakeet sailing a boat. Nor can the child's father. But the very eccentricity of this portrait is its main attraction. What fun it would be to see an angry parakeet flutter and scream, flapping its colorful wings as a big fat carp suddenly appeared from under the water to claim the bird's boat for himself. We share the infectious merriment of the beaver at the sight of the unfortunate bird's treatment by the rude fish, and cannot but enjoy the child's mirth at this highly entertaining melee. Just as a catchy tune can make us feel like bursting into song, so these rhymes inspire us to imagine the scenes for ourselves. Yet rare is the artist capable of capturing the innocent, delightful, and charming mood of these images. Khoka will go fishing in the Cream River. A frog snatched away his rod, a kite took his fish. By which lake does my Khoka bird live? He flies home to me as I call Khoka, Khoka!

We immediately feel like picturing on canvas the details of Khoka's perilous fishing expedition, although we have to admit that we are not as familiar as he is with the Cream River. It is charming to imagine the little boy waiting patiently for a fish to nibble at the bait at the end of a rod four times his length. It is equally enjoyable to picture the consternation on his innocent, anxious face as he attempts to pull the fishing rod from the clutches of an ungainly, beady-eyed frog, while a big kite swoops down and snatches away his fish.

Khoka's depiction as a bird is also quite beguiling. I can imagine a huge lake, the other shore hazy in the distance. On this bank, where the shallow water laps at a mossy rock surrounded by long stalks of grass, our Khoka, in the company of a few cranes and storks, calmly waits on one leg for an unsuspecting fish. Nearby I see a small cottage standing by a rice paddy ripe for harvest. Leaning against the wooden fence of the cottage is an anxious woman calling for her son in the fading twilight of a fall evening.

Astronomers tell us that when they look into outer space they can see areas where gases seem to be gathering to give birth to new galaxies. One detects similar scattered and half-formed masses of poetry in the world of rhymes. There is nothing complex about these accumulations of imagery - like the fluid state of infant, newly formed planets, these poems have yet to acquire their permanent forms. Let me quote one:

"This is great fun, dear, this is great fun, Show me four blacks and I will go along with you." "Crow's black, cuckoo is black, black are swallow tails, But the blackest of all, dear maiden, are your long black tresses."

"This is great fun, dear, this is great fun, Show me four whites, and I will go along with you." "Storks are white, cotton is white, swan is white too, But the whitest of all, dear maiden, are your shell bangles."

"This is great fun, dear, this is great fun, Show me four reds, and I will go along with you." "Rose is red, oleander is red, kusum flower is red too, But nothing is more red, dear maiden, than your hair's red sindur [vermilion]."

"This is great fun, dear, this is great fun, Show me four bitters and I will go along with you." "Neem is bitter, nisunda is bitter, bitter is makal fruit, But the bitterest of all, dear maiden, is living with one's co-wife."

"This is great fun, dear, this is great fun, Show me four colds and I will go along with you." "Water is cold, ground is cold, the mattress is cold too. But the coldest of all, dear maiden, is your heart."

Poets have sung the praises of women in every language and every age, but the simple, unaffected mood that is captured above is rarely encountered in high literature. The unconscious irony of the lines is intriguing. Compared to the tasks demanded of the suitors of Sita and Draupadi, those requested of the lad courting our simple girl are quite easy. Lucky is the man who has only to name four examples of things black, white, red, and sweet from the vast array of things in the world in order to demonstrate his willingness. Men have it easy in these, the last days of the Kali Yuga.

No longer are they required to pass tests of manly valor to claim their women, such as stringing Siva's bow or demonstrating great feats of archery. Instead they demand fat dowries from their fathers-in-law, not the least bit ashamed of such unmanly actions. I much prefer the simple test that the hero of our small poem has to take to win his bride. Although the reader is left in the dark about the outcome, I suspect that our hero must have passed with distinction. His answers were clearly quite satisfactory to the examiner, and I am sure they caused him no difficulty. The test seems to have been almost like an open-book exam, but if it satisfied the examiner then it is not for me to complain.

The maiden starts off by saying, "This is great fun, dear, this is great fun." It is clear that the test has already started, and that the examiner, pleased with the earlier answers, is keen to prolong the test. There seems nothing more pleasant than this. If the composition of this rhyme had been entrusted to us, we almost certainly would not have started off in the middle; we would have been tempted instead to begin with a grand and eloquent introduction. First we would have described an examination hall; it may not have resembled the University Senate Hall, but perhaps the Eden Gardens. We would have further improved the romantic ambiance by adding moonlight, a gentle breeze, and the songs of nightingales.

I suspect, however, that while such arrangements might have increased the grandeur of the occasion, they would have failed to capture the charm of that simple innocent girl whose hair was darker than swallow feathers, whose bangles were whiter than swans, whose vermilion at the parting was brighter than kusum flowers, whose embrace was sweeter than the smile of a child, and whose love was more refreshing than flowing water. A girl so moved by the simple praise of the poet that she was willing to give herself to him would almost certainly have escaped the fetters of our ornate and eloquent composition. We could, if we wanted, polish and rework such rhymes to ready them for publication. We could also read into them somber moral rules and inscrutable philosophical observations. If nothing else we could certainly make them into vehicles of social awareness and modern education. If, for example, we had wished to invite the moon into our civilized company, would we have tempted him with the simple things described in the following rhyme?

Come, come, Uncle Moon, come adorn, Come, dear, and adorn the forehead of my darling baby. I will save you the fish head when I prepare the fish, I will save you some grains when I husk the paddy, I will save you some milk from our black cow, I will save you a bowl to drink from, Come, dear Moon, and adorn my darling.

What sort of moon is being described here? This is the homely moon seen from a Bengali cottage, the familiar Uncle Moon of all Bengali children. This is the moon that glimpses the delight of playful naked babies in the courtyards of village huts through gaps in the leaves of wind-blown bamboos. This moon is the intimate relative of all Bengali families. How, otherwise, could anyone dare to tempt the hero of the night sky, the love-object of the stars and the keeper of the divine ambrosia, with such inconsequential things as fish heads, rice grains, and warm milk? Others might have tempted him with the fragrance and honey of flowers and the songs of nightingales, or with rarer things like sweet dreams, the bliss of love, the longing of the heart, or the innocence of new brides. But the moon would have stayed right where it was.

The rhyme-makers, though, do not tempt the moon with empty promises. To them it is not impossible that the moon might come down to earth and join in the children's play. They are not such cynics. They do not get swayed by the passion of grand poesy, and they do not promise the moon anything they do not themselves possess. Meanwhile, the moon, hearing the innocent calls of the Bengali village households, smiles without committing himself to anything. He even gives the impression that someday, on his way to the eastern horizon, he might make a detour and appear grinning at the doorstep.

I have already mentioned that these rhymes seem like pieces of a lost world. They are filled with the fragments of vanished human emotions. Just as the footprints of prehistoric birds on the shores of ancient seas are seen as fossils with their forms intact, so long-forgotten smiles and tears, and the sadness they contain, are preserved in these rhymes. Age-old human emotions float by on these rhymes, acquiring new life as they touch the feelings of the living and finding nourishment in our tears.

"The sky grows dark on the other side, The rain pours heavily. The pepper tree is filled with red fruits on this shore, Sweet little brother dear, I feel heartsick." "Please somehow stay for another month, dear sister, I will definitely bring you back home next month." "The inner core of my body burns in pain." "Come, O come to the river and drown yourself in the water." Who knows the identity of the young bride who uttered the above lines in the moment of her deepest sorrow and despair? Many similar expressions of sorrow have vanished into the air without leaving a trace. This particular one somehow survived:

The sky grows dark on the other side, The rain pours heavily. One cannot but feel heartsick on such a day. This is how the great poet of the court of Ujjain described it: A sudden cloud can mute the mind of the happiest man - how much more when the one he is dying to hold is far from him.

The emotion that the masterly poet has captured in a sigh has overflowed its bounds in the lines "Sweet little brother dear, I feel heartsick." "The inner core of my body burns in pain." "Come, O come to the river and drown yourself in the water."

Who could ever record all the pain and suffering that burden these lines? The young woman may have been suffering for days in an unfamiliar, unloving household when her dear brother - her childhood playmate - came to visit her. Could she have controlled herself on such a day? Memories of childhood games, of her loving parents and pleasant home, rushed in and no one could stop the emotions from taking over. That day, when the dark clouds gathered on the opposite shore, she felt she could take the pain no longer and wished to take shelter beneath the cool waters of the river.

There is a grammatical error in the poem that I hope the careful editors of Bengali will forgive. By applying a feminine adjective to her brother, the poor girl shows her utter ignorance of the rules of our language. She never imagined that this trivial error would be immortalized, along with her sorrow, in this rhyme. Had she known she probably would have died of shame. The error is not that serious - it is even possible that she was addressing her sister. I would hope that those of my colleagues who, in their concern to preserve the integrity of the language, often sacrifice its many homely charms, yield sometimes to playfulness and indulge in the habit of inappropriately addressing members of the opposite sex as their brothers.

Bengali society nurses a deeply felt wound: that caused by sending our young daughters to the households of their in-laws. As they leave, inexperienced and innocent, to make their homes with completely unknown families, we look upon them with a special, keen tenderness. This heartrending emotion has come to be associated with the Bengali fall festival. This festival honors not only Ambika but our daughters as well, expressing the sweet yet sad love of all Bengali households and lending it objectivity. The welcome songs and farewell songs in praise of Durga voice the emotions of every Bengali mother. This sentiment has also found expression in children's rhymes.

Today is Durga's bridal shower, tomorrow is her wedding, Durga will travel to her in-laws', drowning our sansar [household] in sorrow. Mother weeps, mother weeps on the floor After she has adorned her with a coral necklace. Father weeps, father weeps in the darbar [parlor], He has filled his dear daughter's trunk with money. Aunt weeps, our aunt weeps in the kitchen, This is the aunt who has served her rice on stone platters. Cousin weeps, cousin weeps in the barn, This is the cousin who has served her milk in big bowls. Brother weeps, brother weeps holding on to her sari, He is the one who filled her dresser with clothes. Sister weeps, sister weeps holding on to her bed, She is the one who had once called her a husband-devouring witch.

Before going any further let me just interject a few words. Although the past actions of the sister who now weeps by the bed were not particularly admirable, and although it is of course best if sisters do not fight, still such things happen quite regularly in all households. A gentlewoman should never use inappropriate language in public, but I cannot take too seriously the girl's calling her sister a husband-devouring witch during a fight, given that the harshness of the comment seems far outweighed by the depth of emotion betrayed in the lines above. The bride's mother adorns her with ornaments, her father provides for her future, her aunt gives her meals, her cousin feeds her milk, her brother presents her with clothes; in such a loving family we would naturally expect nothing but the most exemplary behavior from the sister as well.

That is why we are so affected by the final line that describes the sister's past actions. The sadness of the parents is expected, but the grief of the girl who never missed a chance for a good fight is possibly even more heartbreaking. Unexpectedly discovering her tender love for her sister, she bursts out crying by their childhood bed. This must have been the same bed that the two sisters shared when they were young, in the same room that witnessed the two girls playing, fighting, and growing up together. The sister's lonely sobs in this familiar room seem to wash away all the pains of the past.

These rhymes contain huge chapters of our social history in seemingly trivial lines. The next rhyme expresses the age-old concern of all Bengali mothers.

"Swing, dear child, swing With a comb on your red head, Your groom is going to arrive soon, He will take you away in an instant." "Why are you fretting so much and being so unhappy? Think whose house you made your home."

Such thoughts come naturally to a mother as she gently rocks her little girl to sleep. The only solace when in such a mood is the fact that such things have always happened. She herself left her childhood home one day with a heavy heart, but the intense pain of that occasion has now completely disappeared. Her daughter too will leave someday, but again, the pain of that parting will not be permanent.

There are numerous references to Putu's journey to her in-laws' house in these rhymes.

Putu is to travel to her in-laws', Who is going to give her company? We have our tomcat at home, all ready to go along, We shall let them pass through our shady, cool mango groves. We shall provide four strong palanquin bearers. We shall provide four servant maidens to anoint her feet, And we shall have to provide sweet rice puffs to please her mother-in-law.

It is clear from the last line that concern with pleasing mothers-in-law was as intense at that time as it is now. If, however, simple rice puffs sufficed for this purpose in those days then I am sure the parents of many present-day brides must long for that golden age - they are only too painfully aware of the measures needed to please the modern mother-in-law.

The imminent departure of a beloved daughter is not the only reason for sorrow. A far more serious and difficult situation is the marriage of one's daughter to a worthless groom. Often parents, owing to financial concerns or pressures to maintain the family honour, consent to totally inappropriate matches. The pain of such injustices is sometimes expressed in rhymes like the one below. The reader must remember here that all emotions expressed in rhymes are fragmented, a curious mixture of mirth and sorrow.

A bird dances on a pomegranate tree, The drum beats a happy tune. Dear nanny, do you know me? Serve me some rice, please! Annapurna, butter cream, Tomorrow I will go to the unknown house. Their son slapped me on the face, Came weeping to uncle's place. Uncle matched me with an old groom. Dear uncle, I implore you, Get me back to my mother's room. Mother gave me a fancy bangle, father gave me a sari,

Brother gave a hard shove, "Go back to your sasurbari [in-laws' house!." In those days before the rule of British law, responsibility for reinstating marital contracts lay with the relatives and not with the police, and the task had to be accomplished as swiftly and expeditiously as possible. Perhaps the rules of the family were better than those of the court! These days we ask a judge to help restore our legally wedded wives to us; next, perhaps, we will appeal to the governor to solve our marital misunderstandings! Whatever the process may be, it is doubtful that any greater cruelty exists than marrying one's own daughter to a worthless man under the threat of brute force.

Society is quick to forgive the parents' mistakes. The old groom, however, is a constant irritation. The only weapon at society's disposal is biting sarcasm.

The palm tree was cut down at the Bose's household, The maiden is as pretty as Gouri. Destiny gave you an old groom, what am I to do? Bought a conch bangle for you with good money, Gold earrings for the ears, On the day of the wedding noticed an old man with dense beard. Did you chew off your eyes, parents and uncles? You married off your daughter to a tobacco-smoking wretch! His hookah floated away, he died coughing, Shook him a little and found him dead. Lo! As I was draining the rice, he was up and ready to be fed! What treatment for that poor old wretch!

Neither of the two groups of verses above can be faulted for lack of heritage. The heritage of rhymes, however, lies not in their literary pedigree but in the fact. that they are in every age the first expressions of human creativity. They are every bit as fresh on this hot summer afternoon in the nineteenth century as they were at the dawn of human history.

We have yet to talk about the undisputed monarch of the Bengali household: our Khoka and Khuku. Just as the ancient Rgvedas were composed in honour of gods like Indra, Chandra, and Varuna, these rhymes were composed in honour of Khoka and Putu, the two divinities of the Bengali mother's heart. The beauty, cheer, and tender delight in the lines of these new Vedas devoted to children are limitless. The enchanted devotee of the goddess Khuku has fashioned numberless idols of her beloved - the child is looked upon sometimes as a bird and at other times as the moon, a precious gem, or even a flower garden.

I will go away with my beloved to the forest, What should I eat there? I will sit at peace and admire the pretty face of my moon.

There exists nothing as odd as love. Love has accompanied God's creation from the very beginning, yet it always attempts to break the rules of creation. It behaves as though it were a captured bird in the iron cage of the world. In spite of repeated and harsh disappointments it is unable to give up the idea that the rules are easy to break if one wants to - in its awareness of its power to fly it forgets the iron bars of the cage. There is no need to take one's love into the forest as the speaker of the rhyme above wants to; staying home may in fact be far more convenient. It is far more peaceful in the forest, of course, but that's about it (especially when even the speaker acknowledges the possible scarcity of food in such a place). But still love asserts itself and says, "So you people think that I can't do that?" Such rash and impertinent statements manage to distract even wise old men like me! And we do have to admit, "Why not?" Should a mean-spirited realist come along and ask, "And what do you propose to eat there?", love immediately answers, "I shall admire my beloved's face in peace." Statements that would normally seem to be exaggerations, lies, or the musings of a madman are readily accepted when said in a spirit of love.

Another quality of love is that it can magically transform one thing into another. Love refuses to abide by the accepted boundaries of the material world. Readers will have already noticed that it readily transformed a little boy into a bird, and that no biologist expressed concern. Again, when the same child was made into a member of the heavenly family, no astronomer dared voice an objection.

Love asserts itself most in situations where it first carefully builds up an image, then demolishes it with contempt the next moment. The next poem furnishes an example:

Where shall I find the moon, my darling? I cannot make one as it is not made of clay, I cannot pick it like a fruit from the tree, Where am I to find a moon like you? You are the king of the moon, Go to sleep, dear son, go to sleep.

The moon is not within anyone's reach, so these statements are perfectly logical and correct. If, however, one next tells the child that he is the king of the moon, then why bring up all the rational nonsense in the first place?

One comment may not be totally out of place here. The irrationality often associated with women does not reflect any limitation of their intelligence. The world they live in is primarily ruled by love, and love is an inhabitant of Heaven. "Why," it asks, "should anything be more important than me? Why shouldn't all obstacles fall by the wayside simply because I wish them to?" Love still operates by the laws of the heavenly realm. But alas! What could be more irrational than Heaven in this material world? I suspect that the little bit of Heaven still remaining here has been captured by women, children, lovers, and other such highly irrational beings. They often forget that this world is ruled by the laws of matter, and that it is due only to carelessness that bits of Heaven sometimes remain.

Love erases the boundaries between flowers, children, birds, and the moon, but it also draws limits where none exists and creates new forms from nothing. No biologist, for example, has ever attempted to include sleep within the folds of the animal kingdom. But a mother can give sleep a living form simply because it is known to alight on the eyes of her darling child.

Sleep wanders through streets and markets, I bought you for four pennies, come sit on the eyes of my precious darling.

As darkness falls the streets and marketplaces are gradually deserted, and sleep, which freely rested on weary people's eyes during the day, seeks shelter for the night. Possibly that is why it accepted such a low wage from the mother even in these days of high prices.

We are told that the ancient Greeks often personified sleep in their literature. A similar technique was used by the poet

Michael Madhusudan Dutta. Our rhymes appear to be unique, however, in their personification of dance.

Jingle dance jingle. The froth of fig and pakur [a wild fruit]. The bullocks ate the sugar, the goats ate the paddy, Go buy some dance for my precious darling.

And not only that - another rhyme manages to describe a child's every movement as a separate entity:

The dance of the hands, the dance of the feet, the dance of the pretty face, The dance of the gorgeous eyes, the dance of the arching brows, The dance of the perfect nose, the dance of the bending hips, Have you ever heard of any other kind of dance? I found my darling after a lot of sadhan [penance].

Love often sees unity in multiplicity and multiplicity in unity. It can lend magnitude to things that are simple, and change grand things into simple ones. In this poem dance itself is granted an existence independent of the dancer.

The language used in some rhymes also reflects the exalted status of the child.

Khoka will visit the Teli neighborhood. The women there screamed at him, "Who are you, a butter thief?" He broke the pots, finished off the cream, will I ever see him again? If I meet him in the Kadamba grove I will certainly take away his flute.

Here the unconventional but endearing verb form bedu karte is used instead of the regular bedaite, as would have been more appropriate if the intention had been to maintain the integrity of our language. Use of the more ordinary form, however, would most certainly have marred the glory of master Khoka. Bedaite may suffice to describe the walks of the rest of us, but it certainly cannot adequately describe the special charm of Khoka's wanderings.

Khoka has returned from his walk. Cool some milk for him. The milk bowl is hot. Khoka gets mad. Khoka will go sailing with red shoesies on his feet.

It is a big event in the household indeed when Khoka, upon his return home, gets mad because the milk bowl is hot. The circumstances of his expedition to the water are also worth noting. Notice the way Khoka's shoes are described in the last line. Even if we flaunted the best pair of shoes from the most eminent of British merchants, people would still call them shoes. However, the simplest of Khoka's footwear attains the glory of being called "shoesies," simply because they belong to him. Obviously the value of a pair of shoes depends primarily on its owner.

Finally, I wish to direct your attention to one more thing. Man's worship of God finds fruition only in intimate association with human love; love of God becomes real only through love of other human beings. "I gaze at the face of my precious child at peace" - this is ideal meditation. There must be something in the face of a young child that tempts people to leave other things so that they may enjoy it in solitude - it makes the world seem meaningless, a mere distraction from this pure pleasure. Mothers find in the faces of their children the deepest pools of delight, the same delight that tempts yogis away from the lesser pleasures of the material world. That is why the mother in one of our rhymes above sings, "I will go away with my beloved to the forest, what should I eat there? I will sit at peace and admire the pretty face of my darling."

In many rhymes we can see little distinction between human children and the divine child of Devaki. In other cultures such liberties would probably be considered blasphemous. But, I think, to relegate the world of the gods to a place far away from the living and loving world of humans is not only an insult to humanity but contributes little to the adoration of God. In these rhymes the two worlds come together without effort, the portraits of the mortal child and the immortal God magically merging with each other; no one notices when the divine child quietly takes the place of the human child. And when we say of our Khokababu, "If I meet him in the Kadamba grove I will certainly take away his flute," only one who has heard him play can understand how it is that he managed to bring the divine flute from Vrindavan to the Teli neighborhood.

I have compared these rhymes to clouds. Both are ever-changing, both display multitude of hues, and both float about without any effort. Both appear meaningless to us. Rhymes are beyond the regulations of literature, just as clouds are untouched by the rules of meteorology. Both, however, accomplish wonders in our material world. Clouds nourish juvenile plants with their rain; rhymes nurture the infant heart with their rich and loving imagery. It is this freedom from the fetters of convention that enables both to be such sources of delight.

DISCUSSION

Tagore examines three distinct issues in this essay. First is the relevance of these rhymes in the lives of their composers and the significance they have for the narrative community. Although intended for children, the rhymes also express the social concerns and fears of adult females. Tagore thus stresses the importance of community experience in the composition process. Tagore's view of the chhelebhulano chharha as vehicles for unburdening community anxiety resembles the psychoanalytic approach to the interpretation of European fairy tales. But although Freud's ideas have greatly aided folklore research in Europe, their application to non-Western materials has so far been less than satisfactory. An examination of Tagore's rather different analytic approach may thus provide clues for a better understanding of the oral composition process in general, and explain why Freud's theories often prove inadequate for the understanding of non-Western folklore. Freud, for example, noted that uncomfortable social problems are suppressed and as a result surface in folklore in various disguises. Bengali rhymes, however, do not subvert the problem - the fear and sorrow is laid out in the open for all to see, sometimes to the extent of obsession. A similar obsessive concern with women's social problems is seen in the contemporary feminine discourse recorded in ethnographic accounts.

The second issue examined is the nature of spontaneity in oral composition. Tagore cites the phrasing patterns of the oral formulas in rhymes when he links the spontaneous thought of the composition and performance process to the innate rhythms of spoken Bengali. He also emphasizes the importance of wordplay in rhymes, comparing this process to the free association of thought that occurs in dreams (a view reminiscent of the connections drawn by Freud between folklore and dreams). Tagore claims that the composition process for these rhymes is analogous to dreaming because both deal with transitory images reflected on the mind, and because both are directly linked to word association. Tagore thus proposes parallel origins for dreams and folklore in wordplay and the association of thought. This hypothesis provides an alternate to the model of the composition process that links memory with innovative wordplay.

The third issue is the connection of religious and folk themes in these rhymes. The indigenous and community-oriented nature of religion in India has resulted in a very fluid demarcation between folk religion and folklore. This tendency, which is peculiar to Hindu culture, makes it quite difficult for scholars interested in disentangling the two spheres of intellectual activity. For Indians such a merger of religious and lyrical feelings is not awkward at all; it may even be essential for the arousal of the rasas necessary for aesthetic enjoyment. The recognition of the dependency of aesthetic appreciation on specific religious and cultural sentiments may be particularly useful in achieving a better understanding of the worldview of the community from which the lore is generated. This is particularly stressed in Tagore's writing, as a result of his mystic temperament. A clear example is the passage in "Chhelebhulano Chharha" where Tagore refers to the similarity between the fleeting images in the poems and the thought process of children:

> Children are incapable of adhering to such rules - they have only recently arrived from the carefree, cheerful, and impulsive land of the gods. Unlike us, they are not yet used to long periods of servility. The child, building castles in the sand and forming rhyming images in his mind, imitates the actions of our Creator in this mortal world.

This comparison of the carefree acts, or leela, of the Hindu Creator with the acts of children might be hard for readers to appreciate if they do not share the Indian spiritual ethos. Thus before considering Tagore's ideas any further it might be helpful to further clarify the meaning of the word lokashahitya.

This word, often used in Bengali as a synonym for the English "folklore," is a direct joining of the Sanskrit words loka, meaning people, community, and, by extension, society, with shahitya, meaning literature. According to A. K. RAMANUJAN, shahitya suggests a joining together of word and meaning; the term stresses the nature of this relationship and the aesthetic pleasure derived from the interplay of word and meaning in defining the identity of verbal acts of creation.

This is a very different criterion from that used in the West to define literature. One major quality by which literature is judged in the West is its existence in writing, and thus its separation from verbal creations, which are transmitted primarily by word of mouth. The same stress on mode of transmission can be seen in the current popularity of the term "oral tradition" in the literature departments of this country. As we have seen, the distinction between written and oral has little relevance in the Indian context (probably because of the comparatively low rate of literacy). This is why the Ramayana and Mahabharata can move so effortlessly from the high literary to the popular oral milieu.

The term lokashahitya further suggests that it is a kind of shahitya generated by the community or the people. Hence the issues of authorship and individual creativity are of little importance. Moreover, the idea of community-generated verbal creation has a special significance in the context of the Hindu worldview because Hindu belief systems, unlike Judeo-Christian religious traditions, are essentially community-generated. This parallelism in the origins of folklore and religion has made the acceptance of lokashahitya among educated people relatively easier in India than in the West.

A different kind of discrimination, however, works against such literature in India. The association of folklore with regional (and often tribal) cultures is often viewed in a negative light by the classically oriented elite. This factor was strengthened during Tagore's time by the influence of Indian romantic nationalism. The stark marginality of tribal cultures vis-a-vis mainstream Indian society led the Bengali romantics to associate noble simplicity not with the "simple" tribal folk but with women, the other disenfranchised group in Indian society. Tagore's tone in this essay clearly reflects that bias, as when he says, "I suspect that the little bit of Heaven still remaining [in this world] has been captured by women, children, lovers, and other such highly irrational beings." Such blatant sexism was part of the nineteenth-century Bengali Zeitgeist. Ramendra Sundar TRIVEDI'S preface to a later collection of nursery rhymes captures this spirit clearly.

For some time respected Mr. Rabindranath Tagore has expressed a keen awareness of the absence of this kind of collection. A few years ago he read an essay entitled "Feminine Rhymes" at a public gathering.... However, Mr. Tagore did not satisfy himself with merely reading an essay, but involved himself in the collection process. It is due to his efforts that this collection is being published in the quarterly journal of the Bangiya Shahitya Parishat.... I admire the compiler of the current volume as he was not deterred from his so-called childish efforts despite the ridicule of his learned older colleagues.

Tagore's interest in "naive and childish" poems stems from his empathy with the English Romantics. Like Wordsworth, Tagore extols the simple pleasures of the rural population and the intensity of emotion that arises from these pleasures. However, unlike the Romantic poets, who in their efforts to create poetry that imitated folklore ended up composing verses as far as could be from "spontaneous overflows of powerful emotions," Tagore recognizes the essential difference between creative literature and folk traditions, and repeatedly stresses the latter's appeal to our aesthetic sense.

Tagore uses spontaneity as the key to explaining the nature of creativity in oral tradition. According to Tagore, the spontaneous playfulness of these rhymes reflects the absence of any systematic development of thought. Tagore summarizes the contrast between the organized thought process that leads to high literature and the thoughts that give rise to these rhymes: Rhymes, like children, are born naturally of the human mind. This claim is a significant one. Disconnected reflections on the outside world drift regularly across our minds without any conscious effort. They take on different shapes and forms, effortlessly jumping from one subject to another. Just as dust, pollen, smells, noises, leaves, and drops of moisture float aimlessly in the world around us, colors, smells, sounds, fantasies, scattered thoughts, snatches of conversation, and discarded fragments of experience wander randomly through our minds.

When we concentrate our thoughts on a particular topic, however, these excess murmurs cease, these thoughts fly away, these fantasies shatter, and our mind and imagination start flowing in a single stream. Children's rhymes are a product of a different mental state.

The thoughts, sounds, and images that cross our minds when we are in a state of repose continuously change their shape and configuration, like clouds floating in the sky. If these aimless reflections could somehow be recorded on a piece of canvas, we would find some similarity between these pictures and our rhymes. Rhymes are only reflections of our ever-changing inner mind; they are like the fluid shadows of clouds on the clear waters of a lake. This is the reason I say that rhymes are born spontaneously.

Rhymes are products of the part of the human mind that is related to dreams and affect us at a deeper level than conscious thought. Tagore points to the fleeting nature of the images in both dreams and rhymes as evidence that similar mental functions are at work. Describing Shiv Sadagar's snack at his in-law's house, Tagore asks, "Could this be like a dream, with the shalirice chira having somehow changed itself into binnirice khoi between one glance and the next? Who can say that Shivuthakur did not similarly transform himself into Shiv Sadagar?"

On the basis of this rhyme, Tagore further claims that consecutive images in oral poetry are often linked through the association of sounds or words. For example, the natural cadence of the line shali dhaner chira noy re, binni dhaner khoi is maintained by repeating the dh sound twice using the word dhan. These natural rhythms, expressed through such simple alliterative techniques, are easily imprinted on the child's mind and play a vital role in memorization and transmission by attracting attention to certain catchy phrases. Changes in the imagery, too, are dependent on this natural play of sound, which explains the abrupt transformation of images and the preponderance of nonsensical jingles.

Dreams, according to Tagore, follow the same rules of sound association as rhymes; the parallel nature of the mental states that give rise to dreams and to rhymes explains the overall similarity in their forms. Thus Tagore's view of the connection between dreams and folklore rests on quite different premises from Freud's: Tagore explores the possible role of language and wordplay in the development of both processes, while Freud makes dreams and the subconscious the source of folklore. Tagore appears to be linking two important approaches to the interpretation of folklore - the oral-formulaic and the psychoanalytic - in his analysis of rhymes. Interestingly, Tagore's theory places him squarely within the mainstream of the classical Indian literary tradition. An illustrative example is his comment that it is very hard for him to dissociate his childhood memories from the imagery in his favourite rhyme, "The rain falls tip tap, the river gets flooded." These lines bring back images he probably visualized when he first heard the poem. Thus certain sounds became permanently associated with certain images.

These few lines were like the classic epic Meghaduta to me at that time. I could vividly see a majestic, heaving river rushing downstream on a dark and stormy day. I could also see a few small boats moored by the bank and the three new brides of our Shivuthakur busy preparing the evening meal.

Such scenes are familiar to anyone who grew up on the Gangetic plains of Bengal. Through his description Tagore attempts to strike a sympathetic note in the minds of his readers, who recall similar emotions. Thus the line transcends the immediate scene described, and, through sympathetic resonance in the mind of the audience, stimulates the recollection of similar scenes. The enjoyment derived from such recollection then reinforces the lines in the memory and paves the way for their further transmission. In this way these poems become part of the community and cease to be the poet's personal property.

This view of verbal composition is essential for understanding the concept of rasa, as it is more conducive to the appreciation of community-generated verbal creations than to the products of the individual imagination. How similar is the above description to what Richard BAUMAN describes in his analysis of verbal performance.

In an artistic performance of this kind, there is something going on in the communicative interchange which says to the auditor, "Interpret what I say in some special sense; do not take it to mean what the words alone, taken literally, would convey." This may lead to the further suggestion that performance sets up, or represents, an interpretive frame within which the messages being communicated are to be understood, and that this frame contrasts with at least one other frame, the literal.

Thus Tagore's comment,

How am I, an aged, somber, and status-conscious man, to capture the soft, loving, and simple voices that are eternally associated with the telling of these rhymes? I fear that readers will have to contribute that tender essence from their own childhood memories. With what magic can I bring back the love, the tunes, the memories of softly lit evenings with which these rhymes are linked? I can only hope that at least some of that charm has been captured in the following lines, could be intended to draw his readers into a shared supraliteral interpretive frame.

However, Tagore's emphasis on spontaneity in the composition process presents a problem. He claims that these poems are the products of spontaneous thought, while at the same time recognizing that it takes serious effort to make a poem appear spontaneous. If these poems are conscious creations, then the spontaneity is not sincere. According to Tagore, the spontaneity of these children's rhymes is similar to the mood of playfulness in children's games. The rhymes and the games both are results of passing fancy and devoid of any grand forethought, the innate free-floating quality of both is the source of their attraction. He writes:

The mind of the child, however, is for the most part free of such conscious rigor. The child is affected independently by his own imagination and by the outside world; one arrives after the other. The fetters of the conscious mind are distressing for children; they find it difficult to pursue anything along a well-defined path of cause and effect. Children build castles in their minds just as they build sand castles by the shore. Sand lacks the ability to stick together, so the castles are not solid. But it is precisely this quality that makes sand suitable for the creations of children. One can build a grand structure in minutes with fistfuls of sand, and if the architecture turns out not to be to one's liking one can easily correct the mistakes. The playful creator, when exhausted, can instantly level the structure with a kick and happily return home. When one builds by design, however, one is forced to follow the rules of building. *However, Tagore also says:*

The reader must remember that one cannot deliberately create a dream. The rhymes above may have been written effortlessly under the impulse of carefree fancy, but such a sense of the carefree cannot be consciously captured. We have conditioned ourselves to conscious and directed effort, and thus simple and natural things have become terribly difficult. A mood of anxious stress shadows all our efforts even when totally uncalled for. The moment such feelings make their presence felt all carefree impulses and fancies congeal and lose their freedom to fly. That is why I maintain that those who are able to compose children's rhymes do it naturally, while those who have to make the least bit of effort find the task impossible.

Since these rhymes are products of the playful mode of the mind, an analysis of children's games provides a way out of Tagore's problem. Brian SUTTON-SMITH'S analysis of play is helpful in this regard.

For me play is what a person does when he can choose the arbitrariness of the constraints within which he will act or imagine. In its most primordial form, it is an attempt to control the circumstances of habitual action by reversing the direction of control.... The player substitutes his own conventions and his own urgencies for those of society and nature.... Once play has commenced, however, even this play "set" can be put to one side. Perhaps play itself can become taxing, the players often seek further excitement in breaking it down. Thus, after a long period of concentrated block building, the young associates will gain great enjoyment from destroying their own efforts. What we describe as playfulness is often a state in which a further escalation of "sets" takes place and the play involvement gives way to wild invention, hilarity and sometimes complete nonsense.

What Sutton-Smith describes as the escalation of the "play set" may appear arbitrary to those not in tune with the play mode, but can be a source of pleasure for children and adults alike. It appears that the adult composers of chhelebhulano chharha may have capitalized on this arbitrary quality in composing these poems. And in a traditionally male-dominated society where women are the caretakers of children, who else but women would be more aware of this balance of control, and in a better position to play with it?

Though these poems expertly mimic a child's sense of logic, the contents reveal the voice of women composers. The majority of them reflect a Bengali girl's fear of the unfriendly and often cruel household of her in-laws. The system of negotiated marriages and patrilocal residence, which does not allow prior contact between the bride and the groom, gives rise to great anxiety in the minds of adolescent girls. The poems consequently acquire an immediacy in the lives of the women listeners, who in turn act as the main transmitters and retainers of the rhymes.

Finally, Tagore directs our attention to the explicit religious overtones of many of the rhymes. The lines, "Today is Durga's bridal shower, tomorrow is her wedding/Durga will travel to her in-laws', drowning our sansar in sorrow," reflect more than the general melancholy associated with the final day of the annual festival of Durga. The Hindu myth of the wedding of Himalaya's daughter Uma (an incarnation of

Durga) to Siva has been annexed by Bengali folklore, which has transformed Uma into a simple village maiden married to an older, indifferent husband. The festival of Durga is seen by the community as the time when Uma - like all married daughters in Bengal - can spend a few days at her parent's house. Thus the myth reflects an immediate social reality. Here the personal (and even community) concerns of Bengali women transcend their limits through their connection with the general religious sentiments of all Bengalis. Thus the creator of this rhyme manages to impart a universal pathos simply by using the name Durga.

Similarly, the worship of the divine child Krsna by his mother resonates through poems that on the surface have no religious connotations. By using certain formulaic descriptions closely associated with Krsna, such as calling the child a butter thief, the creator of the folk rhyme manages to arouse a feeling of bhakti and tenderness among adults. Thus these rhymes very cleverly manipulate classical traditions in ensuring their own popularity. Tagore's interest in folk traditions and folklore was that of a creative artist.

Many of the issues that he commented upon have recently emerged as important in current folklore scholarship, while others reflect then-fashionable views on folklore. However, for me the charm of Tagore's writing lies in the way it arouses feelings of nostalgia for a place and time to which I no longer belong, but to which I feel connected. His work is thus immensely pleasurable for me.

Myths of Poesis, Hermeneusis and Psychogenesis: Hoffmann, Tagore, and Gilman.

By Lansing Evans Smith

The myths of the maze, the goddess, and the descent to the underworld play a key role in the "Mines of Falun" by E. T. A. Hoffmann, "The Hungry Stones" by Rabindranath Tagore, and "The Yellow Wallpaper," by Charlotte Perkins Gilman. All three works present images of women imprisoned within a labyrinthine underworld that represents the threat of madness; and in each case the myths become metaphors for poesis, hermeneusis, and psychogenesis. While the three myths are archetypes frequently found in world literature, it is rather rare to find them so intricately combined to fashion a complex allegory of writing, reading, and the birth of the self.

In Hoffmann's "The Mines of Falun," Elis, the romantic protagonist, descends into the mines of the Metal Queen, lured downward by the mysterious old miner, Torbern, who leads him through a "gate" ("dem Tore") on the road to the mines. Torbern is what van Gennep would recognize as a threshold guardian, and what Karl Kerenyi would call a "Seelenfuhrer"—or psychopomp. As such, Torbern is associated with doorways (archaic icons of liminality and descent), which lead to the entrance to the mines. Elis stands in between identifies (sailor and miner, bachelor and husband), drifting in a marginal limbo, literally "standing at the door," neither in nor out.

Though initially afraid to go down into the "hell like abyss" of the mines, Elis follows Torbern bravely to "the enormous gulf, like the jaws of hell itself," from which stupefying vapors rise, as if from a "hell-broth... brewed down below". He compares the mine entrance to the place where "Dante went down and saw the Inferno"; the miners themselves look like "diabolical creatures". When Elis first goes down to work in the mines, the "uncanny" Torbern appears like a "black shadow," to strike his hammer with the force of "distant thunder," before disappearing "amongst the black labyrinths of the chasms". Later Elis sees the "desolate crags" at the entrance to the Inferno as a "numberless horde or horrible monsters, the dire brood of hell".

Hence, Hoffmann's evocation of the underworld draws from Dante, Norse legend, and classical mythology: Torbern is a Virgilian guide, leading Elis into the Inferno; he is a type of Thor, swinging his hammer to strike fire and thunder; and he is a type of Hades, albeit servant to his Persephone, the Metal Queen who rules down below, and to whom Elis is irresistibly drawn.

For the labyrinthine underworld of the cave is also the archetypal domain of the Earth Goddess. Eliade suggests that the cave was assimilated to the labyrinth and the goddess from prehistoric times: "To penetrate into a labyrinth or cavern was equivalent to a mystical return to the mother" ("Terre-Mere" 75; my trans.). By the same token, the "ores extracted from mines are in some wɛ ys embryos", and "the kiln where enameling material was smelted (schmelzofen) was designated by the name of matrix or maternal bosom (Mutterschoss)". Hence, Elis ultimately collapses into the arms of "the mighty queen" of the caves, who draws him "to her breast".

The alchemical dimensions of mining and the imagery of the Great Goddess emerge later in the story, when Elis resolves on his marriage night to go down into the caves in order to retrieve the "queen's heart," which he imagines as a "glorious red carbuncle" that is the maternal source of all "hearts and souls". Like the image of the Goddess herself, the metallurgical operations leading to the forging of the philosopher's stone in alchemy are natural symbols of creative processes of poesis, a point Joyce would later make clear in A Portrait of the Artist as a Young Man, which closes with Stephen Dedalus's resolving to "forge in the smithy of my soul the uncreated conscience of my race". Other feminine symbols of creativity in "The Mines of Falun" include the notions of cooking and brewing (the vapors rising from the "hell-broth" brewed down below), old Germanic symbols of the union of the loving and terrible aspects of the Goddess to be found in, for example, "Hansel and Gretel," or in the image of the "Black Witch" ("Schwarze Kochin") in The Tin Drum by Gunter Grass.

As Eliade notes, "The comparison of human work, in which fire was used (metallurgy, forging, cooking, etc.), with the growth of the embryo inside the mother, still survives, obscurely, in European vocabulary (cf. Mutterkuchen, placenta, Kuchen, gateau)". Hoffmann emphasizes the erotic, creative symbolism of the caves and the Metal Queen by surrounding her with "innumerable beautiful maidens" from whose hearts roots, plants, and metal flowers grow.

A similar complex of images linking the maze, the goddess, and the underworld is to be found in "The Hungry

Stones" by Rabindranath Tagore, whose fusion of realism and folktale in the stories of 1890s looks forward to T. S. Eliot's notion of the "mythical method" of 1923. The symbolism of the descent to the underworld (the nekyia) begins with the "nightmare" and "weird fascination" the protagonist experiences in "the solitude of the deserted palace". The solitude is inhabited by the "invisible" shades of the Persian past—harem girls flitting among the fountains, corridors, staircases, and river palisades of the ruins of the palace, which is some 250 years old.

It is the land of the Persian dead, and many of the archetypes of Hades surface in the narrative: in addition to the icon of the ruined mansion inhabited by the ancestral shades (cf. Dante, Virgil), there is the river crossing (de rigueur for the nekyia since Gilgamesh, Odysseus, and Dante), the tortuous ascent of stairways, and the ensuing passage through doors, corridors, and chambers, which is as characteristic of the maze as of the underworld (cf. "The Descent of Inanna" or the Egyptian Books of the Dead). This passage gives the protagonist access to an "intangible, inaccessible, unearthly vision", as he treads the pathways of a "bewildering maze of alleys in the enchanted dreamland of the nether world of sleep". As in both "The Mines of Falun" and "The Yellow Wallpaper," this netherworld is inhabited by a woman who lures the hero or heroine more deeply into her labyrinthine realm, and seems to demand the heroic task of liberation.

In "The Hungry Stones," the protagonist hears the harem girl calling at "dead of night" from "below the stony foundations of that gigantic palace, from the depths of a dark damp grave". Tagore conflates the imagery of the maze, the underworld, and the goddess in this as in many other passages in the story: beneath the stairs, "the doors and windows and corridors and verandas and rooms" and the "vast desolate hall" through which the protagonist wanders, far below the palace in her "dark damp grave", the goddess lies in prison. Like the Gnostic Sophia, imprisoned in the labyrinthine underworld of matter, or like the Hindu jiva, trapped in that realm of illusion (maya), which is generated and sustained by fear and desire (kama-mara), the harem girl longs for release The story is replete with archetypal symbols of her creative and destructive power: rose water fountains and clear water reservoirs; "joyous maidens" who evoke the nagas of Hindu folktale and myth; the gurgle of springs "gushing forth in a hundred cascades" that suggest the goddess is the source of life; the new moon and bright star reminiscent of the archaic affiliation between such goddesses as the Sumerian Inanna and the Greek Aphrodite with the planet Venus; the passionate "pain and craving and ecstasy" of the beloved suggesting her erotic fascination; and the feeding of fruits and wine symbolic of the mother archetype, which is both nurturing and devouring, "loving and terrible".

The palace itself as "living organism slowly and imperceptibly digesting" him suggests the devouring aspect of the mother archetype, who is both "Muse" and "witch", and whose attendant reptile is also typical: a "mysterious serpent" twisting her "stupefying coils" around the hapless protagonist. She is finally a "famished ogress" eager to swallow him up, like the Hindu Goddess, Kali

The configuration linking the maze, the goddess, and the underworld in "The Hungry Stones" is archetypal: the Malekulan myth of the descent, for example, revolves around the encounter with a Devouring Ghost, who sits beside a cave and stone, with which she is identified (a hungry stone!), and who traces half of a maze in the sand at her feet, which the peregrine soul must complete in order successfully to navigate the passage to the afterlife.Numerous Bronze-age funerary monuments consist of huge stones engraved with spiral labyrinths at the entrance to such tombs of the Goddess as the ones to be found on Malta, in the Mediterranean, or at Newgrange, in Ireland and the oldest myth we know tells of the Goddess Inanna passing through the seven labyrinthine gateways of the underworld. From such preliterate roots, the imagery of the maze, the underworld, and the goddess gradually emerged as metaphors of the intricacies of reading and writing in the literary tradition: Penelope Reed Doob has delineated the development of the myth of the labyrinth from

Ovid to Chaucer; J. Hillis Miller has applied the metaphor of the maze to narratology; and, more recently, I have shown how these three archetypes serve as tropes of poesis and hermeneusis in Modernism.

The same basic archetypal configuration is found in Charlotte Perkins Gilman's "The Yellow Wallpaper"—though with a twist. The narrator's breakdown and deepening depression lead to a journey by boat to an old rental home where she is to undergo a rest cure. Several broadly folkloric motifs associated with the other world surface during her stay in the ruined rental home, such as the mushrooms she sees in the wallpaper (universally present in such fairy tale illustrations of forest journeys as Ivan Bilibin's picture of Baba Yaga for the tale of "Vasilisa the Beautiful") and the host of "creeping women" held behind the wallpaper by an uncanny spell (like the enchanted ladies in Castle of Marvels in Wolfram's *Parzival*). The "night-sea journey" through the underworld —a characteristic image of the descents of Gilgamesh, Odysseus, Aeneas, and the Ancient Mariner—comes full circle at the end of the story, when the narrator says, on the last night of her rest cure, that the family will "take the boat home tomorrow".

Other motifs of the descent to the underworld (doorways, eyes, sisters, and the spouse substitute) take us back further in time, beyond the male journeys, to our oldest archetype of the nekyia—the Sumerian "Descent of Inanna," from about 1750 BCE In that tale the female protagonist, Inanna, descends through a labyrinthine series of seven gateways to stand naked in the presence of her sister, Ereshkigal, the Goddess of the Sumerian underworld, who fastens the "eye of death" upon her. Inanna's corpse is then hanged for three nights upon a peg (the first crucifixion! And of a female—not a male—divinity), before Inanna is resurrected by the bread and water of life, to return home to her husband, Dumuzi. Dumuzi is knocked off his throne and eventually sent down to the kur himself. The archaic iconography that links doorways, the maze, the eyes of the great goddess, and the underworld in this myth is one of the most widespread characteristics of the

Mediterranean during the Bronze Age, abundantly illustrated by the anthropological meditations of Lawrence di Stasi, and the archaeological studies of Marija Gimbutas.

All of these archetypal motifs occur in "The Yellow Wallpaper." The protagonist hallucinates "strangled heads and bulbous eyes" and the "faint figure" of a mysterious woman behind the "florid arabesque" of the yellow wallpaper. As she descends more deeply into the "sub-pattern" of the labyrinthine paper, she becomes imprisoned by her efforts to liberate a mysterious woman, so much so that, when her husband arrives on the morning of her departure, she says, "I have locked the door". He calls for his sister, Jennie, to bring an axe "to break down the beautiful door"; then he says, "very quietly indeed, `Open the door, my darling!'". She tells him that there is a key "by the front door," and, when he retrieves it and enters the room, he stops "short by the door," and then faints, horrified by the sight of his wife crawling amidst the wallpaper on the floor.

I emphasize this drama at the doorway here (in which the word "door" occurs six times) for its archetypal nature, evoking as it does a long lineage of mythological, literary, religious, and folkloric prototypes that link doorways, the maze, and the descent into the underworld. In the numerous paintings of the Harrowing of Hell—those by Durer and Brueghel, for example—Jesus stands at or passes through a sequence of arches and doorways to liberate Eve (and Adam) from Hell. Gilman's Eve, however, thwarts the harrowing and resists patriarchal liberation, preferring perhaps to remain within the domain of her newly discovered Self. For "The Yellow Wallpaper" is very much a story about psychogenesis, about the creation of a new identity. It charts a Jungian discovery of the Self, a movement toward wholeness achieved through the ordeal of the individuation process—hence the activation of the archetypal motifs associated with the nekyia, which emerge spontaneously during periods of transition and crisis.

But "The Yellow Wallpaper" is also an allegory of poesis and hermeneusis, a metaphorical image of the writing and interpretation of texts: for the protagonist spends a great deal of time "reading" the wallpaper, and this activity catalyzes her writing the story. There is a kind of hermeneutic circle at work here. Like the wallpaper—composed of sequences of "lame uncertain curves for a little distance" that end suddenly in "suicide" —the story is composed of sequences of very short paragraphs (sometimes eight in a row composed of single sentences). The effort of the protagonist as a "reader" of the paper's "florid arabesque", a hermeneutic act that leads to her activity as a writer. Her task is to trace the "pointless pattern to some sort of conclusion," and to discover its "principle of design," which looked at one way seems to violate all the laws of "radiation, or alteration, or repetition, or symmetry," and hence to be "a kind of `debased Romanesque' with delirium tremens, consisting of "isolated columns of fatuity". But from the diagonal perspective, the floral patterns connect in a consistent (if horrifying) "optic horror, like a lot of wallowing sea-weeds in full chase".

The quest for one's destiny, for the shape and significance of history and the cosmos, is, of course, one of the standard themes of the descent into Hades—Odysseus talks to his mother there, who reveals what lies ahead for him in Ithaka; Aeneas talks to his father, who discloses the imperial destiny of Rome; and Dante talks to those souls who reveal the essence of Providential design. Hades may even be etymologically linked to the notion of pattern or design, since the epithet "aidoneus" connects with "eidos," the Platonic term for form. But for Gilman, the primary tenor of the metaphorical descent has to do with the creation and interpretation of a new kind of text, one that has a "pattern" or "sub-pattern", let's say, if not strictly speaking a "principle of design". Like the woman in the wallpaper, Gilman must "shake the pattern" of traditional patriarchal symmetries, in order to create her own voice and feminine sense of literary design. She does so by re-visioning the oldest of all literary patterns—the descent to the underworld.

In this respect, Gilman's version of the nekyia has much in common with those of Hoffmann and Tagore, both of whom employ the archetypes of the descent, the maze, and the goddess as metaphors of psychogenesis, poesis, and hermeneusis. In "The Hungry Stones," the protagonist (Mr. Collector or "Srijut So-and-So," as he calls himself) discovers a postcolonial identity that transcends the boundaries of the Raj. He says that he could discern, amidst the "curious apartments" of the ruined Persian palace, "the fragments of a beautiful story, which I could follow for some distance, but of which I could never see the end".

Like the curved lines of the yellow wallpaper, these "dream fragments" suggest the endless lines of a story of which the protagonist must seek the conclusion; and, as in "The Yellow Wallpaper," the story concerns an abused, elusive, and imprisoned woman whom the protagonist must liberate. He can only do so in a story that is replete with birdsong and supernatural music, conventional symbols of poesis. Amidst the vast and desolate corridors of the palace, the protagonist hears "a strange tune on the guitar... the distant note of nahabat... the song of the bulbuls... the cackle of storks in the gardens, all creating round me a strange unearthly music". The songs transform Mr. Collector "into some unknown personage of a bygone age, playing my part in unwritten history" —"unwritten," but sung, dreamt, and intimated by the act of poesis, which the supernatural tunes of birdsong and wailing woman compel, so that the story becomes itself an act of hermeneusis, an interpretation of the birdsong.

As a traditional symbol of the "angelic language" of in the Koran, or in such texts as Farid Attar's Conference of the Birds, the birdsong suggests a divine dimension of the "unwritten history" that Srijut's descent compels him to tell. The bulbul is Keats's nightingale, traditionally found in Persian poetry. But the inarticulate wailing of the Arab girl's ghost infuses the story with a demonic undercurrent. In addition to the birdsong, he must translate her "hard, harsh, mirthless laugh," and her "violent wringing sobs".

The song of the bulbul and "the passionate cry" of the madwoman compel the Collector to tell his tale—rather like the Ancient Mariner's encounter with the Spectre Woman on the Ship of Death does—but in order to do so, the protagonist-as-poet must become a protagonist-as-reader and "hear the history of a young Persian woman who once lived in that pleasure-dome". Although the Collector fails to liberate the woman from her ghostly hell, he succeeds in bringing back a powerfully suggestive story: his descent catalyzes an act of poesis, as he tells his tale in the train station.

We find a similar conflation of the acts of psychogenesis, poesis, and hermeneusis in "The Mines of Falun." For amidst the "richest veins" of the bottomless caves ruled by the Metal Queen, Elis comes to assume that "none but he understood the secret signs, the significant writing, fraught with hidden meaning, which the queen's own hand had inscribed on the rocks, and that it was sufficient to understand those signs without bringing to light what they indicated". The problem is simultaneously one of psychogenesis, in which old persona dies so that a new self may be born; of hermeneusis, which requires understanding ("verstehen") the "secret signs" of a "significant writing" ("die geheimen Zeichen', die bedeutungsvolle Schrift"); and of poesis, for the story gives us a glimpse of the "the queen's own hand" engraving ("hineingrabe") the sacred symbols of the underworld on the parchment of her preference ("Steingekluft," clefts in the rock). The fact that Elis dies in the labyrinthine underworld of the Queen suggests the difficulties Hoffmann had (throughout his career) in reconciling his poetic with his domestic concerns: it seems the husband must die so that the poet may be born.

The German word for writing in this passage preserves the same pun we have in English (engrave): "Grab" of course means grave, as in tomb, and "graben" can mean to dig as well as to engrave. The word "hineingrabe" is therefore resonant: it signifies engraving letters into stone or metal, digging into the earth, and, oddly enough, the process of "going into" ("hinein") a grave ("grabe"). The same pun emerges at the end of the story, where Elis links the Metal Queen with a "cherry-coloured sparkling almandine, on which the tablet of our lives is graven". The word for her writing on the tablet is again "graven". To engrave suggests a process of memorializing, and the underworld has traditionally been conceived of as what MacDonald calls "the burial place of memory." By this curious twist of language, Hoffmann strikes upon the term for writing that links poesis and hermeneusis with the descent to the underworld, very much in the way Thomas Mann would later do, in the "Prelude" to Joseph and His Brothers, in which he compares the "Feast of storytelling" to the "descent into hell", and in The Magic Mountain, in which Naphta says that the grave "comprehends all hermetics," and that it is the "crystal retort wherein the material is compressed to its final transformation", a trope powerfully present in "The Hungry Stones" and "The Yellow Wallpaper" as well. All three works, in fact, use the mythic descent into the maze, in which a powerful image of the feminine is imprisoned, to figure the dynamics of creativity: a new story, a new interpretation, and a new self are all born from the madwoman in the underworld.

Readers interested in literary adaptations of these three myths (and others) will find chapters devoted to them in my books on modernism (Rape and Revelation, and Ricorso and Revelation), postmodernism (Figuring Poesis), and world literature from antiquity to the present (The Hero Journey in Literature).

Intersecting Nationalisms

By Philip Holden

IN HER INTRODUCTORY study Colonialism/Postcolonialism, Ania Loomba notes that the epithet "postcolonial" can now be attached to almost any object from home furnishings to novels, having acquired something of the range of "ethnic" in popular vocabulary. In this light, a book covering the years 1890-1920 which presents its subject matter as "postcolonial" might be the cause for some alarm. Elleke Boehmer's Empire, the National, and the Postcolonial is in fact a timely work, and indeed part of a growing and welcome movement towards historicization in postcolonial literary studies. Commencing as a challenge to categorizations such as "New Literatures in English" or "Commonwealth Literature" in the 1980s, postcolonial studies from its inception attempted to make connections across diverse geographical areas and between different literary genres. Much early postcolonial criticism, however, tended to impose its own binary logic: it either celebrated contemporary texts as emancipatory examples of postcolonial literatures in English, or deconstructed canonical European texts written under colonialism as representative of the prison house of colonial discourse.

Boehmer's study, in parallel with recent publications such as Robert Young's Postcolonialism or Simon Gikandi's work on Jomo Kenyatta, attempts to engage with the complexity of resistance and nascent nationalism in the colonial world, and their expression in textual form. Her study thus elaborates an early phase of "cross-nationalist" connections between various actors who imagined—and indeed laid the foundations for—national communities, utilising an "interdiscursive" methodology that emphasizes both historical actions and their mediation through a variety of literary and non-literary texts.

After a brisk and competent survey of relevant work in the field, Boehmer's introductory chapter concludes with a discussion of Irish nationalist opposition to enlistment in the Boer War, and the parallels drawn in the pages of the weekly review United Irishman between two very different anti-colonial struggles. The following two chapters of Empire, the National, and the Postcolonial illustrate connections between Bengali and Irish nationalism through a detailed exploration of the relationship between Sister Nivedita (Margaret Noble) and Aurobindo Ghose. Chapter 4 then turns to Sol Plaatje, the South African writer and political activist, his engagement with thinkers as diverse as W. E. Du Bois and Mohandas Gandhi, and his resultant production of "polyphonic" writing in both his novel, Mhudi (1930) and his nonfictional work Native Life in South Africa (1916).

In a final chapter, Boehmer is more discursive, drawing together two discussions that address the relationship of modernism to anti-colonial nationalism. In the first of these, she explores the influence of Rabindranath Tagore on W. B. Yeats, while in the second she examines how the writing of

Leonard Woolf on colonial Ceylon, especially his novel The Village in the Jungle, recognizes, albeit obliquely, "the claims of native self-representation" and produces a form of "symbolic decolonization."

As this summary indicates, Boehmer makes no attempt at comprehensiveness—in the manner, for example, of Robert Young's recent volume—but rather proceeds with a series of case studies. This allows at times for considerable depth of analysis, but the paucity of the studies themselves, and the considerable variation in the detail in which they are presented, do tend to leave some of Boehmer's larger claims unproven. The weakest of the studies is also the longest—the discussion of the relationship between Nivedita and Aurobindo, which constitutes almost one half of the length of the book. Somewhat recursive in structure, Boehmer's account never quite pins down the nature or the significance of the "cross-cultural interaction" between her two political and social activists.

She largely uses secondary sources, admitting that connections between the two are "difficult to trace, being either deliberately obscured or, very often, unreliably recorded." Her exploration raises many more questions than it answers. Boehmer rightly notes that Nivedita's relationship to Irish nationalism, as an English-identified Protestant, was tenuous, but the result of this revelation is to direct discussion away from "cross-nationalist" connections to the manner in which anti-colonial nationalism in Bengal mobilized and rewrote Orientalist stereotypes in order to produce a distinctively Indian modernity. Unfortunately, this is ground already picked over by seminal writings in the postcolonial studies canon: the influential historical and theoretical work of Partha Chatterjee and Dipesh Chakrabarty, for instance.

Lacking the ability to work with Bengali language sources, and indeed relying substantially on secondary sources such as biographies, Boehmer tends at times to move away from analysis to description. Two possible strategies which serve her well later in her book—the use of archival material, or the close analysis of a single text using the methodologies of literary criticism—are not applied here. The reader waits for detailed analysis of how Nivedita's and Aurobindo's texts work as cultural artifacts, but most of Boehmer's close reading, when it does occur, is concerned merely to show mutual influence. Many fascinating topics are raised in passing—Nivedita's identification with Kali, for instance, or the production of an aggressively masculine Hinduism to oppose the feminisation of Indian cultures under colonialism. However, Boehmer never moves far enough away from summary to explore in detail the manner in which these strategies become embedded in individual texts: "interdiscursive" methodology here has neither the rigor of history's attention to primary sources, nor the depth of rhetorical and semiotic analysis associated with literary and cultural studies.

Boehmer's chapter on Plaatje suffers none of the limitations of its two predecessors. It focuses, initially at least, upon a single text, Native Life in South Africa, and applies close literary analysis to its "multitextured, tessellated style," exploring parallels with contemporary metropolitan writing while simultaneously registering the limitations of those comparisons. From this initial discussion Boehmer moves to examine pan-Africanist connections in other writing by Plaatje, and the manner in which the particular inflection of his nationalism prevented him from making what might, with the benefit of hindsight, seem an obvious political alliance with Gandhi and the Natal Indian Congress. Her emphasis is on tracing back the complexities of Plaatjee's ideological beliefs from the "heteroglossic eloquence" of the surface of his writings, and she does this skillfully, pointing out Plaatje's complex negotiation between complicity with and resistance to colonial power—his "often openly contradictory, ambivalent, and restlessly shifting allegiance."

The discussion of Plaatje also provides a useful bridge from political writings to anti-colonial politics embedded in more overtly literary production. Boehmer's final chapter commences with a discussion of the interconnection of modernism and anti-colonial nationalism at a time of perceived imperial decline. Of her two case studies here, that of Leonard Woolf seems closest to conventional colonial discourse analysis. Boehmer's reading of Woolf's novel, and his short story "Pearls and Swine, "is usefully informed by study of his letters home from Ceylon, which map out a growing awareness of the moral contradictions and absurdity of colonial administration. Woolf's growing awareness of other cultural world-views, Boehmer argues, results in a text which recognizes the limits of its own efforts to represent Ceylon, and also leads less directly to both the author's anti-imperial political and economic writings and to his wife Virginia Woolf's modernist critique of British middle-class society. In her second case study, Boehmer focuses on Yeats' introduction to Tagore's 1912 translated volume of his own Bengali poems, Gitanjali. If Yeats indulges in an Orientalist production of Tagore as a representative of an Asia marked by a "fuller, vibrant, and more unselfconscious life," he also discovers in Gitanjili "Ireland's dream self," an ability to retrieve a past uncontaminated by colonialism that can fortify the nation as it awaits independence.

Empire, the National, and the Postcolonial is certainly more ambitious than its author's earlier, excellent introductory text, Colonial and Postcolonial Literature: Migrant Metaphors, but it lacks the coherence of the latter work. Boehmer's study is valuable in the way it foregrounds neglected texts, and suggests new possibilities for reading and novel critical perspectives on late-nineteenth and early twentieth-century literatures in English. Yet one wishes for more, and more precisely focused case studies. The book maps out a huge canvas and then works in detail—and with mixed results—on a few areas of it only, leaving the rest unfinished: one would wish for at least a series of complementary, congruent images, if not for a full picture.

Interpreting Tagore's Gitanjali

Thanks to the wonderful professor who taught us Tagore's Gitanjali, I was able to discover a whole new world. Being a poet myself, I do dream a lot but the Gitanjali transported me to heaven! The amount of peace one can receive by going through its verses is truly ineffable. Tagore, I believe, is simply great...I had written an essay in which I'd given an original interpretation to the Gitanjali as I had understood it. This piece is a long one but I hope lovers of poetry would take some effort to read through the same and communicate their feedback. Gitanjali- A Poet's Prayer

There is a distinct spiritual flavour to the verses of Gitanjali. Going through them, anyone is capable of getting transported into -what in poetic idiom is often referred to as- a 'poetic heaven'. As Yeats too had expressed, in his introduction to the Gitanjali, the verses depict a poetic world which can only be dreamt of by most of us. There is an other-worldly feel to it. These words can only be uttered by a person who has transcended the physical world to explore what lies beyond it. But isn't that what every poet wishes to achieve? Gitanjali is labeled as 'religious' poetry by critics; but to Tagore these verses were just poetry and it is these classic poetic qualities of Gitanjali that is dealt with presently.

Even a lay reader with no feel for poetry will be able to recognise how these verses though framed in the simplest of vocabulary, manage to articulate thoughts and feelings of the highest order. To comprehend them may not be possible for all. Such is the talent of Tagore and such his inspiration. In Gitanjali, I see a poet's gratitude finding expression. Every single utterance of the poet is soaked in this gratitude felt towards that Supreme Being without whose will, a poet would never have been born. The very fact that God has appointed him to accomplish a poet's task is elevating. And when the recesses of a poet's mind, impregnated with divine feelings, reach the state of maturity, it is but a moment's labour for a poem to be born through the channel of language.

To a true poet, every poem comes as a blessing granted after numerous prayers have been offered at the altar of the Supreme Being. Gitanjali is an embodiment of these several prayers that the poet has offered at the feet of the divine giver of inspiration. While praying, we do not always plead for something, sometimes we praise our God and sometimes we just share our sorrows and joys as if talking to a friend. At other times we simply meditate in order to compose our minds. Prayers are means to achieve inner harmony. The quality of poetry depends upon the intensity of this prayer. Tagore's Gitanjali is evidently a prayer, a poet's prayer, and manifests in itself that harmony which the poet has experienced.

A proper prayer is that which involves direct communion with the Supreme Being. It is an extremely personal experience. Therefore the poetic inspiration experienced by a poet is also a thoroughly personal experience, which one can consider as the benefit of prayer. In Ramayana we do see how Ravana through constant utterance of prayers wins the favour of Lord Shiva. We can consider a poet too to be like that, who constantly prays for inspiration and when the Muses are convinced of his sincerity the wish is granted.

Since we are considering Gitanjali to be the poet's prayer, we must understand that it is something which the poet has undergone singularly. The tapasya (spiritual endeavour) of the poet can not be therefore understood by all. One must have experienced the same to be able to interpret exactly as to what the poet is saying. Yet an attempt is being made here to interpret the Gitanjali from the point of view of the poet's various poetic experiences and the poetic qualities that the song exhibits. The very opening line of Gitanjali reflects the inner harmony that the poet has experienced. The words are an outburst endeavouring to articulate the intense pleasure that the poetic experience has conferred upon him:

"Thou hast made me endless such is thy pleasure"

'Thy' here becomes poetic inspiration itself and 'thou', the one who inspires. Anyone is bound to be ecstatic if his prayers are answered. We see the poet here starting at the peak of inspiration. In the life of every genuine poet such a moment does occur when he experiences endlessness.

One may wonder how endlessness can be experienced in a brief moment as it is seemingly contradictory. This can be explained by drawing a parallel. Coleridge in his Kubla Khan talks of 'A sunny pleasure domes with caves of ice'. Here the opposites merge and all seemingly contradictory elements are resolved. When a poet touches this point he experiences eternity for in a state of eternity only a single entity exists. It is only when the poet attempts to articulate this oneness that he has experienced by means of language that the problem arises. Because language and words belong to the mortal world; their realm is the world of corporeal experience. There is no specialized vocabulary that can articulate abstract, extra-sensory experiences such as what a poet experiences when he is inspired. At the level of experience, everything is in a state of unity. But the moment a poet descends to the ordinary mode of existence and tries to express in finite language his infinite experiences, the contradictions emerge.

In prayer, it is essential to keep in mind that we are insignificant as against the Supreme Being. It is important therefore to develop a humble attitude. A humble being who is completely aware of the all-encompassing spirit of the divine being would always express a state of wonder, awe and admiration at this. There can be no room for the poet's vanity to exist when he is subject to the 'grandeur of divine inspiration'. A true poet who experiences intense divine inspiration would sublimate to an egoless state and he will humbly follow the instructions of his Muses:

"My poet's vanity dies in shame before thy sight. O master poet, I have sat down at thy feet. Only let me make my life simple and straight, like a flute of reed for thee to fill with music."

The poet here confesses how his own vanity or pride dies in shame when he realises that there is a poet more powerful than himself now before his sight. There is no way in which he can surpass the 'master' poet, and it is only within his capacity to surrender at his feet and endeavour to emulate him. The expression 'master poet' also needs some explanation here. The Supreme Being who bestows poetic inspiration upon man is a poet himself, his creation being the universe. We have earlier reflected upon eternity and oneness of experience. The same idea continues here. The master poet, who is the creator of the universe, is one single entity. The music that emerges from the master poet is responsible for the creation of this universe. The poet is only an instrument, like a flute, and it is the divine giver of inspiration who fills it with music. The poet knows that it is only as an instrument that he must ideally come before his master's presence:

"I know that thou takest pleasure in my singing. I know that only as a singer I come before thy presence."

Also note these lines:

"I know not how thou singest, my master! I ever listen in silent amazement.

The light of thy music illumines the world. The life breath of thy music runs from sky to sky. The holy stream of thy music breaks through all stony obstacles and rushes on.

My heart longs to join in thy song, but vainly struggles for a voice. I would speak, but speech breaks not into song, and I cry out baffled. Ah, thou hast made me captive in the endless meshes of thy music."

The poet's constant reference to music and singing must be commented upon. What possible connection could there be between poetry and music? Apart from both being forms of art, the aspect of metre, rhyme and coherence of thought in poetry relates it to the rhythm found in music. Metre, rhyme and coherence of thought in poetry bring in order and discipline and to achieve this is no mean task; the poet will have to struggle. A poet will have to constantly endeavour for this and the task in hand cannot be finished so easily. Music suggests euphony as against cacophony which can be related to the assonance in poetry as against the dissonance of the world. Musicalisation of the poet's thoughts would result in harmony in his poetry, which is an essential attribute.

Tagore's reference to the master poet's music and his own music also relate to 'musica mundana', the harmony of the elements of the spheres and of the seasons, and 'musica humana', the harmony between body and soul in singing, respectively. As mentioned earlier the divine giver of inspiration is a creative being as well responsible for the creation of the universe and the harmony found in it. The poet on the other hand is also creative and creates art and gains inspiration from the master forever emulating him. A poet experiences meditative immersion in music always in the consciousness due to the fateful participation of the celestial sphere; his sensitivity is integral. In the universe a mortal being always sees contradictory elements. The life-giving breath of the master poet is boundless and capable of inspiring all but only the ones gifted with the faculty for it can benefit from the inspiration. When the poet reflects upon how the master poet went about creating the universe from all the dissonant elements that were present he is awe-inspired, his own task of composing poetry from life seems insignificant and all that he can do is but to listen in silent amazement. And when a poet transcends his mortal being and merges with the divine, even if it is only for a brief moment, the apparent discordance dissolves, there is clarity of vision and he is able to see the 'uni'verse as opposed to the 'multi'verse.

Philip Sidney in his 'Apology for Poetry' echoes something similar when he says, "The world of nature is brazen but the poet always delivers the golden." Due to the profound inspirational heights a poet is able to universalize and make one what is otherwise harsh and separate. "All that is harsh and dissonant in my life melts into one sweet harmony- and my adoration spreads wings like a glad bird on its flight across."

As mentioned earlier, at the peak of inspiration every poet experiences oneness. The poet when inspired is able to compose harmony out of dissonance and make soft what to a layman appears harsh. Only an artist is gifted with the faculty by which he can make dead stones come alive, and convert them into an idol for worship. We all do see stones lying on paths trodden upon day after day, but how many of us do recognize that these stones can become objects of worship when carved? That is exactly what a poet does. Even Shakespeare echoes this idea when he says "through indirections find directions out." The raw material for poetry is the world and its life which is physical and short-lived but the poet composes life into poetry, casting it in the mould of inspirational experience and takes it to metaphysical heights and makes it everlasting. That is why when the poet is inspired all the harsh and dissonant elements in life melt into one sweet harmony and flow out as poetry. This also explains why all great poets harp on the significance of coherence, wholeness of meaning and comprehensiveness of imagination in poetry.

In the line quoted above, the imagery of a bird in its flight suggests the idea of 'poetic flight'. At the level of inspirational experience a poet is glad and filled with adoration or respect for his Muses. His faculty of imagination is like the wings of a bird that helps him to soar above the ordinary plane of existence and see those aspects of life which others cannot. Keats expresses something similar in his 'Ode to a Nightingale' when he says that he would fly on the "viewless wings of poesy". The authenticity of the poetic experience is established here as other poets have also felt the same way.

But the lack of inspiration or inability to write poetry, also referred to as poetic lull can be an extremely painful experience for the poet, which Tagore expresses in his prayer:

"Away from the sight of thy face my heart knows no rest or respite, and my work becomes an endless toil in a shoreless sea of toil."

The poet's poetic endeavour constantly needs the inspiration of the master poet and away from him the poet would never be able to accomplish his task. The poet's work is no mean task, as already mentioned. Therefore in a situation where there is nothing to inspire a poet has to struggle. In one of the lines previously quoted the poet expresses how when his speech breaks not into song, he cries out baffled. The poet has to communicate his feelings to the rest of the world in a meaningful fashion and this becomes an endless toil in a shoreless sea of toil if no inspiration enlightens him. But the poet is ready to wait sincerely for the moment of inspiration to arrive:

"In the night of weariness let me give myself up to sleep without struggle, resting my trust upon thee. Let me not force my flagging spirit into a poor preparation for thy worship.

It is thou who drawest the veil of night upon the tired eyes of the day to renew its sight in a fresher gladness of awakening."

A sudden understanding seems to dawn upon the poet that his master only wants him to rest for sometime and get back to his task at a later time. The night of weariness can refer to the moments of poetic lull, in which case the poet must sleep or rest, reposing faith in his master that he would awaken the next day with fresh inspiration that would provide him gladness. A poet can never force poetry out of him. Infact it is believed that it is not the poet who writes poetry but poetry that writes the poet. Tagore here echoes something of the same when he says that his own flagging or waning spirit should not make vain attempts. The poet's poetry is the prayer that he offers for worship to his master and a devoted poet can never afford to compromise in his quality of offering. There are other verses in Gitanjali too which echo this idea. Infact if we read the different lines of Gitanjali closely it is possible to relate to similar ideas; only the metaphor varies but the poet's various experiences that find expression would be more or less similar. Take a note of this:

"On many an idle day have I grieved over lost time. But it is never lost, my lord. Thou hast taken every moment of my life in thine own hands. Hidden in the heart of things thou art nourishing seeds into sprouts, buds into blossoms, and ripening flowers into fruitfulness.

I was tired and in my idle bed and imagined all work had ceased. In the morning I woke up and found my garden full with wonders of flowers."

We can connect these lines to the ones quoted earlier. When the poet experiences a lull and is unable to carry forward his task any further; he faces a block. The poet knows that he is a mortal being and his life on earth is brief and the task in hand enormous. He values time and cannot afford to let go even a single moment waste. A poet experiences boundless joy in accomplishing his task but being idle is disheartening and he grieves over time lost when he was making futile attempts to compose poetry. But the poet realises that the moments were not really lost and his master had taken it up from him in order to let him prepare himself. This idea holds relevance because every time a poet experiences spells of lull it only means that his thoughts are undergoing a transformation or renewal of some sort and once they are fully prepared the poet regains his capacity to express them. It is the master that nourishes 'seeds' of thought in the poet's mind and when the poet is able to fructify them into lovely poems he offers them to his master in all obeisance. The poet's poetry is nothing but prayers dedicated to the master poet:

"From the words of the poet men take what meaning pleases them; yet their last meanings point to thee."

Tagore had always maintained that his religion was a poet's religion. Most critics interpret Gitanjali from a solely religious point of view. This maybe because he belonged to an Indian Hindu community generally considered to be pious and devotional. Tagore's poetry cannot be confined to a particular creed or faith; it belongs to the universe.

A poet's religion knows no boundaries, it is all-inclusive. The religiousness of a poet arises not from the religion he belongs to but out of a respect for life which in him is an instinct.

Can anyone ever point out exactly where from faith emerges? It is as impossible as to predict when exactly the heart began to beat or the universe was set in motion. When Wordsworth referred to poetry as the "spontaneous overflow of powerful emotions recollected in tranquility" he fore grounded the word 'spontaneous' only in order to stress on the instinctive nature of poetry writing. The urge to write poetry is a call of the conscience, an intuitive pursuit which not everyone is capable of committing oneself to.

In the essay called 'The Poet's Religion' Tagore says: "Through creation man expresses his truth; through that expression he gains back his truth in its fullness. But the poet in man knows that reality is a creation, and human reality has to be called forth from its obscure depth by man's faith which is creative. The great world... has its call for us. The call has ever roused the creator in man, and urged him to reveal the truth, to reveal the Infinite in himself."

There is mystery in it, like the mystery about life and its depths can never be fathomed using language as a measure:

"At the immortal touch of thy hands my little heart loses its limits in joy and gives birth to an utterance ineffable."

Here the giving birth to an 'utterance ineffable' by the poet is akin to Wordsworth's 'spontaneous overflow of powerful emotions'. When poetic inspiration touches the poet, his sensibility is stirred; the humble poet is elevated to unprecedented heights of imagination in his moments of tranquility and the poetry which overflows or is born out of him then is filled with emotions or joy; guided by his inspiration, he utters what would otherwise be ineffable or inexpressible.

This takes us to another level of understanding of the poet's creed which requires him to utter what under ordinary circumstances is inexpressible. Every religion has its prescribed rites and rituals. A poet's religion also requires him to follow certain methods. "When thou commandest me to sing..." says Tagore which we can relate to the commandments in the Bible that every believer will have to abide by. A poet- if he is a strong believer in his poetic creed- will have to obey the commandments of his Muse, the supreme being that inspires. It is a poet's duty to articulate the truth without being misled into fallacies. That is why poets are believed to be the conduits through which God reaches common man. In his essay, 'Silent poet, untaught poet', Tagore makes an important statement with regard to the poet's rites that must be performed faultlessly:

"A powerful imagination does not by itself make a poet. It must be a trained and refined imagination of a high order. There should be the intellect and the taste to employ the imagination to good purpose." He even goes on to say later, "The imagination too, like everything else, requires training. An imagination without proper training revels in the extravagant, the impossible, the preternatural." He goes on to compare such an imagination with a mirror of curved surface that shows its image disproportionately and then accuses people with ill-trained imagination, "People of such imagination cobble together ill-sorted objects and produce a monster. They are incapable of seeing incorporeal dimensions in a corporeal object..." Therefore a poet has to develop a religious discipline in order to reach that state of perfection. Praying for inspiration, offering one's songs to the 'divine giver of inspiration' and constantly training oneself for the complex art of poetry writing are the rites that a poet must faultlessly perform. It is not an easy path to pursue:

"It is the most distant course that comes closest to thyself, and that training is most intricate which leads to the utter simplicity of a tune."

CONCLUSION:

There is only a very thin line that separates poetry from spirituality or religion. Infact poetic experience is akin to spiritual/religious experience when the poet is genuine in his pursuit. In spirituality great thoughts realised by enlightened beings gradually transformed themselves into religious doctrines and the spiritualist came to be regarded as God incarnate. A true spiritualist never abandons the world but moves along with the world understanding the problems of humanity, redressing them. The poet who experiences true inspiration is also an enlightened soul. He does not shut his doors to the outside world but refines the world through his imaginative capacity and offers the world an antidote for its maladies through his works. A spiritualist conveys himself to the rest of the world by means of sermons and teachings whereas a poet leaves his thought behind in the form of his art. The poet's soul is connected to the divine force, whereas his physical self is linked with the people in the rest of the world and for him complete bondage/surrender to the Divine force means complete freedom where he becomes a tool in the hands of the divine forces. For both the spiritualist and the poet Deliverance lies not in renunciation of the world but in such bondage:

"I feel the embrace of freedom in a thousand bonds of delight." The medium of language has its own impact. In poetry, the spiritual aspects are subtly woven; the poet never preaches overtly. These lines of Tagore directly appeal to his master conveying what a struggle it is for a poet to be able to express satisfactorily in language what he has experienced at the spiritual level. A poet can never completely transfer his experiences into words and the relationship that he shares with the divine forces remains a mystery forever:

"I put my tales of you into lasting songs. The secret gushes out of my heart. They come and ask me, 'Tell me their meanings.' I know not how to answer them. I say, 'Ah, who knows what they mean!' They smile and go away in utter scorn and you sit there smiling."

Infact when spiritual truths are written down they become literature automatically. Take the Bible for instance; today its popularity in the world is more as a literary account of the Christian civilization and its beliefs than as a holy or religious text. Literature, especially poetry, is therefore a viable medium for communicating truths that people realise through heavenly inspiration at various points of time in their life. A poet too is a spiritualist who undergoes a grand transformation in his lifetime due to the various inspirational experiences and becomes sublime. A poet is like the legendary white swan which is believed to take only the milky portion from the milk leaving behind the water in it; he offers to the world pure truth which is soiled by the world otherwise.

Through Tagore's Gitanjali we can get a glimpse of the poet's true nature and his spiritual feelings. Embodied in this work is his very soul; it will continue to give out sparks of truth to the world. This pious poet's prayer will continue to kindle in generations of poets the desire to lead a life of humility and self oblivion and accomplish their task of telling this world what it would not realise otherwise with utmost sincerity. Tagore's own reflection upon his poetry, I suppose, would be the best way to conclude this essay that is all about the poet's prayers leading to divine inspiration and complete surrender to the 'master' poet:

"When I look back and consider the long, uninterrupted period of my work as a poet, one thing appears clear to me that it was a matter over which I had hardly any authority. Whenever I wrote a poem, I thought it was I who was responsible for it, but I know well today that this was far from the truth. For in none of those small individual poems was the real purport of my whole poetical work wholly significant.

What the real purport is I had no knowledge of previously. Thus, without being aware, of the Ultimate, I have continued adding one poem to another. Whatever limited idea I may have ascribed to each of them, today, with the cumulative aid of all my poems I have come to realise, surpassing each of their individual meanings, one supreme and unbroken idea had flowed steadily through them all, so that years afterwards I wrote:

What is this game ever-new
You play with me in your jesting mood?
Whatever I may want to say
You do not allow me to express.
Residing in the innermost me
You snatch words from my lips
With my words you utter your own speech,
Mixing your own melody.
What I wish to say I seem to forget;
I only say what you want me to say.
In the stream of songs
I lose sight of the shores."

Chapter 10

Reviews

Rabindranath Tagore: The Guru of Indian Poets During the days of freedom movement, several poets and writers of India produced creative works capable of inspiring nationalism and patriotism among the people. Among the poets Rabindranath Tagore was a great Indian poet, who contributed enormously to the nation's freedom movement. The Guru of Indian poets, Rabindranath Tagore was born in Calcutta on 7th May 1861. The Tagore family had a long tradition of culture and yet was not closed to the new winds coming from the west to India at that time. And what is more, the family was ready to provide its children every thing that was congenial to the flowering of their inherent talents.

Rabindranath Tagore ran away from a traditional school during his early teens and had his education seen to and supervised by his father. He was sent to England in 1878 for further education under Henry Morley at London University College. At thc threshold of his youth, he had already been initiated into Indian classical literature, Indian and western music and had begun to write verse. In his making as a poet, Tagore was greatly influenced by the inspirations from Brahmo Samaj. His books of poems, dramas, short stories and novels in Bengali soon gave him a distinctive place in that literature. Initially a raconteur, his compendium 'Letters from a Sojourner in London' which was based on his life and times in London was published in book form in 1881. During the same year he wrote the play 'Valmiki Prativa' and it was a rare stage appearance when Tagore appeared in the title role. Tagore's genius entered a new phase when he composed the poems of

'Manasi', the musical play 'Mayur Khela' and the drama 'Raja Rani'. He was the editor of the monthly magazine 'Sadhana'. He ultimately published his works 'Sonar Tari' and 'Panchabhuta' in the same journal. It is the powerful patriotic spirit of Tagore's literary works that brought him in the mainstream of the freedom struggle and earned him national wisdom. He captured the depth of the nation's feelings in his poem 'Into That Heaven of Freedom' a poem that moved many nationalists to tears. Where the mind is without fear And the head is held high, Where knowledge is free, Where the world has not been broken up, Into fragments by narrow domestic walls, Where words come out from the depth of truth, Where tireless striving stretch its arm towards perfection, Where the mind is led by thee into ever-widening, Thought and action into that heaven of freedom, My Father, Let my country awake.

As a patriot poet and a nationalist, Rabindranath Tagore influenced not only the leaders of the national movement but also the masses. His works generated a spirit for liberating India from colonialism. He was on a poetic mission to save India from slavery. His works ignited passion and united people to dedicate themselves to the national struggle. He opposed the Partition of Bengal along communal lines and resented the concept that would divide his beloved state. He preached swadeshi, composed soul-stirring songs, wrote incisive essays, addressed meetings and led protest marches. Tagore gifted to India her national anthem, a prose paraphrase of which he read at Over Town Hall as part of his world famous essay 'My Interpretation of India's History.

The national anthem was composed for the Brahmo Samaja anniversary in 1912. The inspiration and patriotic spirit generated by this song was considerable and immeasurable. The song generated a sense of national unity during the days of freedom struggle which made India stronger than ever before. That poem made one of the makers of modern India. He was a seer and national builder. He was given importance for revival of Hinduism. Tagore was a great poet. In 1874 his first poem 'Abhilash' was published in 'Tattobodhini Patrika'. During his life his entire writings include 1000 poems, 2000 songs and large number of short stories. In 1912, Tagore sailed for England, where the translation of the 'Gitanjali' (Song-Offerings) created a literary sensation among the British poets. Gitanjali established Tagore as a world poet. In 1913, Tagore's Gitanjali was nominated and selected by the Swedish Academy for the Nobel Prize for literature. For his literary activities, he was Knighted by the British government in 1915. But protesting the Jallianwalabagh tragedy, Rabindranath Tagore gave up his 'Knighthood' in1919.

During this time he declared, "When the badges of honour make our shame glaring in their congruous context of humiliation, and I, for my part, wish to stand, shorn of all special distinctions, by the side of my country men who for their so called insignificance are liable to suffer degradation not fit for human beings." Rabindranath Tagore had started his own school at Shantiniketan in West Bengal in 1901, which grew up gradually to be named as the Visva- Bharati or the centre of the world learning in 1971. The place is now one of the recognized Universities of India and has been a place especially for the study of art, music, literature and cultures of the world. Today this university at Shantiniketan sought to provide a place where children could grow up in freedom, amidst an environment of nature's beauty and warm human relationships.

Tagore was not only a good litterateur, but also was a good painter. In his time each painting of his life was very individualistic. He had given tunes to his songs and having a style and a nuance of their own, they form now a separate category in Indian music called Rabindra Sangeet. Tagore was a pioneer in the experiment with rural reconstruction in India. The contribution of his songs to the national freedom movement was immense. In short, he is an example of the multifarious ways the excellence hidden within a person can express itself, provided the proper environment is there and provided the centre within the individual is awake to take advantage of that environment.

To conclude, Tagore's life time achievements can be put in Iqbal Masud's words "In Tagore we have a culture going back 2000 years-it is what one can call the Hindu Culture. But a point that is often missed is that Tagore was a product of the Bengal Renaissance, which in turn was a product of 19th century liberalism." Pradeep Kumar Gan is a scholar of History, Culture and Archaeology, presently at Fakir Mohan University, Vyasa Vihar, Balasore.

Chapter 11

Film Adaptation

1961, India. Documentary, 54 min, B/W
Credits
Producer: Films Division, Govt. of India
Script. commentary & Direction: Satyajit Ray
Cinematography: Soumendu Roy
Editing: Dulal Dutta
Art Direction: Bansi Chandragupta
Music: Jyotirindra Moitra
Cast
Raya Chatterjee, Sovanlal Ganguli, Smaran Ghosal, Purnendu Mukherjee, Kallol Bose, Subir Bose, Phani Nan, Norman Ellis

Summary

The documentary details the life and work of the celebrated Bengali writer Rabindranath Tagore (1861-1941). He was awarded the Nobel Prize for Literature in 1913 "because of his profoundly sensitive, fresh and beautiful verse, by which, with consummate skill, he has made his poetic thought, expressed in his own English words, a part of the literature of the West." Rabindranath Tagore was the youngest son of Debendranath Tagore, born in Calcutta. He was educated at home. At seventeen he was sent to England for formal schooling, which he did not complete. Tagore was knighted by the ruling British Government in 1915, but within a few years he resigned the honour as a protest against British policies in India.

The documentary was made to celebrate Tagore's birth

centenary in May 1961. Ray was conscious that he was making an official portrait of India's celebrated poet and hence the film does not include any controversial aspects of Tagore's life. However, it is far from being a propaganda film.

The film comprises dramatized episodes from the poet's life and archived images and documents.

Comments

The dramatized sequences of boy Rabi (Rabindranath Tagore) and young Tagore in his twenties are moving and lyrical. Ray has been reported to have said, "Ten or twelve minutes of it are among the most moving and powerful things that I have produced".

Awards

- President's Gold Medal, New Delhi, 1961
- Golden Seal, Locarno, 1961

Special Mention, Montevideo, 1962

Bibliography

Rabindranath Tagore by Krishna Kripalani (1962);

Rabindranath Tagore by H. Banerjee (1971);

Rabindranath Tagore by B.C. Chakravorty (1971);

An Introduction to Rabindranath Tagore by V.S. Naravene (1977);

The Humanism of Rabindranath Tagore by M.R. Anand (1979);

Rabindranath Tagore by S. Ghose (1986);

The Unversal Man by S. Chattopadhyay (1987);

Sir Rabindranath Tagore by K.S. Ramaswami Sastri (1988);

Gandhi and Tagore by D.W. Atkinson (1989);

Rabindranath Tagore by K. Basak (1991);

Rabindranath Tagore by E.J. Thompson (1991) Suom.: Tagorelta on myös suomennettu draamat P*imeän kammion kuningas ja muita dramoja*, novellivalikoima *Ahnaat paadet* sekä teos *Puutarhuri* Eino Leinon käännöksenä 1913.

Dutta, Krishna & Andrew Robinson (1995) *Rabindranath Tagore:The Myriad-Minded Man*, London: Bloomsbury.

Kripalani, Krishna, *Rabindranath Tagore* (1980) Calcutta: Visva-Bharati. O'Connell, Kathleen (2002) *Rabindranath Tagore: The Poet as Educator*, Calcutta:Visva-Bharati, 2002.

Tagore, Rabindranath (1980) *Our Universe*. Translated by Indu Dutt. Bombay: Jaico Publishing House

Tagore, Rabindranath (1961) *The Religion of Man*. Boston: Beacon Press.

Tagore, Rabindranath (1985) *Rabindranath Tagore:Selected Poems*. Translated by William Radice. Harmondsworth, Middlesex: Penguin Books.

Tagore, Rabindranath (1966) *A Tagore Reader*. Edited by Amiya Chakravarty. Boston: Beacon Press.